BORN TO RUN

THE RACING GREYHOUND
FROM COMPETITOR TO COMPANION

BY RYAN H. REED

A THOROUGHBRED TIMES BOOK®
An Imprint of BowTie Press®
Lexington, Kentucky

Andrew DePrisco, June Kikuchi	**EDITORIAL DIRECTORS**
Amy Deputato	**SENIOR EDITOR**
Jarelle S. Stein	**EDITOR**
Jennifer Calvert	**ASSOCIATE EDITOR**
Elizabeth Spurbeck	**ASSISTANT EDITOR**
Véronique Bos	**SENIOR ART DIRECTOR**
Karen Julian	**PUBLISHING COORDINATOR**
Tracy Burns	**PRODUCTION COORDINATOR**
Jessica Jaensch	**PRODUCTION COORDINATOR**

Photographs © 2010 by Ryan H. Reed
A Thoroughbred Times Book®
Copyright © 2010 by Thoroughbred Times Company, Inc.

A Thoroughbred Times Book®
An Imprint of BowTie Press®
Thoroughbred Times Company
2008 Mercer Rd.
Lexington, Kentucky 40511
www.thoroughbredtimes.com

Library of Congress Cataloging-in-Publication Data
Reed, Ryan H., 1968-
    Born to run : the racing greyhound from competitor to companion / by Ryan H. Reed.
        p. cm.
    Includes bibliographical references and index.
    ISBN 978-1-59378-689-2
  1. Racing greyhound. 2. Greyhound racing. I. Title.
    SF429.G8R425 2010
    798.8'5--dc22

                                        2009050555

Printed and bound in China
16 15 14 13 12 11 10 1 2 3 4 5 6 7 8 9 10

Contents

Dedication

For my sweet Toolie.

My lucky star fell the day you came to me. We did everything
together, and how I adored you. Now, all these years later,
if I could tell you just one thing, it would be that my chest
became a vacuum the day you left.

May 23, 1986 – January 5, 2000

Acknowledgments

Like most large-scale research projects, this book could not have been realized without the continued support of many friends and backers. Janice Mosher, an adoption volunteer with Greyhound Pets, Incorporated, and a close personal friend, helped in countless ways throughout the entire effort. Gary Guccione, executive director for the National Greyhound Association, made arrangements for me to visit breeding farms near Abilene, Kansas; explained the history of the sport; and assisted in a great many other ways, too numerous to list here. At the Greyhound Hall of Fame, Ed Scheele and Kathy Lounsbury helped supply historical information.

The lion's share of statistical background information for individual Greyhounds was provided by Greyhound-Data.com, a free Web site with information—including race history—compiled by teams of aficionados from Australia, New Zealand, Europe, and the United States. Without the Greyhound-Data Web site and the hard work put into its database by tireless volunteers, it would not have been possible to provide such detailed information about the racing and retired Greyhounds portrayed in this book.

In August 2002, I had the great fortune to be befriended by Vera Filipelli, the director of media relations at Derby Lane racetrack in St. Petersburg, Florida. She and her husband, John, made a trip to Derby Lane feasible for me by insisting that I stay at their home for a week to offset some of the costs. Afterward, Vera continued to help in more ways than I can enumerate here. Simply put, without Vera's unwavering support and friendship, this book would have been much smaller in scope and size; in fact, it might not have been completed at all.

With Vera's help, I got in touch with the Rhode Island Greyhound Owners Association (RIGOA), which generously awarded me a grant that allowed for a trip to Lincoln Park. While I was photographing matinee races at the racetrack, my camera body suffered a catastrophic failure, putting a halt to any further photography. In a near panic, I called RIGOA president Richard Brindle and vice president Dan Ryan, who immediately offered to pay for a new camera body. They are two of the most benevolent men I have ever met.

Later, in December 2005, I received yet another generous grant for my work, this one from the Texas Greyhound Association (TGA). While in the famed Lone Star State, I had the opportunity to document the TGA-owned schooling racetrack in Bruceville; a Greyhound breeding farm; and the Gulf, Corpus Christi, and Valley Greyhound Parks. The kindness and professionalism of TGA executive director Diane Whiteley and TGA executive assistant Lois Mowery exceeded my wildest expectations. Without the RIGOA and TGA grants, the Rhode Island and Texas chapters in this book would not exist.

Other types of valuable assistance were provided by Don Conatser, Judy Enyard, Maurice Flynn Jr., Jim Gartland, Cheryl Gilson, Rory Gorée, Herb "Dutch" Koerner, Patti Lehnert, Connie Loubsack, John Manning, Charles Marriott, Craig Randle, Steve Rose, Ann Waitley, and Carl Wilson. Countless others contributed in valuable ways to this book project. Without their collective support, *Born to Run* would never have become a reality.

Finally, I would like to express my deepest appreciation to my parents, John and Rosemary Zimmerman, who never lost faith in my ability to complete this project.

Preface

The seeds of this book were planted in the Pacific Northwest some twenty years prior to its publication. In 1989, at twenty years old, I realized that something was missing in my life—companionship. After visiting a friend who had just adopted a black Lab puppy, I realized that I needed a dog.

Having never adopted a dog before, I realized I needed to do some research. I turned to the local library, searching through its books to gain any tidbits of information I could. After browsing through the small selection of dog books available, I pulled out an encyclopedia and looked up the word *dog*. A full-color insert showed illustrations of every dog breed. In the most defining moment of my life, my eyes slowly wandered to the Greyhound illustration, which depicted a weird-looking, aerodynamic creature. That casual glance would profoundly change my life.

When my older brother heard about my new interest, he suggested that I call the Coeur d'Alene Greyhound Park in northern Idaho for information. His college roommate was a regular patron and had once mentioned something about adopting a retired racer

Illustrating a sharp contrast in design, Toolie's (R's Snowbird-SC, CD) streamlined profile counters the rigid lines of an old steam locomotive in a Potlatch, Idaho, city park.

from there. That was the first time I had ever heard about Greyhound racing. I called the racetrack the following morning and was referred to the Greyhound Pets of America's Idaho chapter in nearby Post Falls. When I explained to the adoption volunteer what kind of dog I was looking for, she replied, "Oh, I've got a pup that would be just perfect for you. Her name is Toolie." I later visited the racetrack, where Toolie had once greeted patrons, and saw how much the trainers enjoyed being around the dogs and how well they cared for them—the affection was genuine.

A few months after adopting the white-ticked beauty, I joined the adoption group and set out to find as many homes for retired racers as I could. In my first six months, I placed a dozen retired racers and was subsequently voted onto the board of directors at the age of twenty-one. For years afterward, I served the adoption organization by handling media relations, conducting home visits and interviewing potential adopters, providing long-distance transportation, managing a weekly Greyhound get-together, and even repossessing a retired racer here and there for various reasons. While I maintained an interest in learning more about the sport of Greyhound racing, nearly all of my firsthand experience with Greyhounds came from the realm of adoption.

When I adopted my second-generation pups, Dino and Abby, in April 2001, I began to chat with other adopters on Internet discussion boards. I quickly discovered that people had incredibly strong opinions about racing, but when asked how many racetracks or breeding farms they had been to, the answer was almost always, "None." I was struck by the fact that a person could have such strong feelings about something he had never seen for himself. I remembered dogs coming into our adoption kennel who were happy, healthy, bouncing, and acting like everyone in the world was their best friend. I knew that if the dogs were indeed universally mistreated, as some people claimed, they would require a great amount of behavioral modification before being released to adopters. But the dogs went happily into adopters' homes, often immediately after retiring from racing. This is what made me think about doing a book about Greyhound racing and adoption—I needed to see for myself how these dogs lived before they arrived for adoption.

I started the book project in the summer of 2001 in an effort to travel to and gather information on racetracks, breeding farms, and adoption organizations across the country as well as to learn the history of Greyhound racing in America. The first racetrack I approached was the Multnomah Greyhound Park, located in Portland, Oregon. I came with no references and could not even say I knew anyone in racing, yet they gave me full access to the racetrack and allowed me to photograph anything I wanted to. My first thought was, "Incredible! Not only do these people have absolutely nothing to hide, they're extremely proud of what they are doing."

I next traveled to the National Greyhound Association facility in Abilene, Kansas, and visited several other racetracks located in Colorado, Kansas, and Iowa. I had not previously met Gary Guccione of the NGA, yet he took half a day of his own time to arrange several farm visits for me. I told him I had been an adoption volunteer in the past, and that was good enough for him. Craig Randle, the NGA's chief farm inspector, drove me from farm to farm, answering questions along the way.

From 2002 to late 2005, I continued to visit racetracks in Florida, Rhode Island, Texas, and again in the Midwest. I began to see the book project as a work on Greyhound racing and adoption in America, and I set out to expose every nook and cranny with my camera and my pen. What I saw along the way were healthy and happy-go-lucky Greyhounds. Every dog acted as though I were his long-lost friend. My own dogs acted as though every breeding farm they visited was their old home. I had never seen them so happy before— or so disappointed when the visits were over.

During the years I was conducting my research, I began to realize that there was a family environment within Greyhound racing that was separate yet overlapped with the family of those in Greyhound adoption. It also became apparent to me that Greyhound breeders were not in the business for mere profit. They were a collection of people who simply loved being with the dogs. A breeder in Oregon once told me, "If I were to put the same amount of effort into any other business than raising Greyhounds, I would be a millionaire!" I realized that there was no chasm between racing people and adoption people. They stood on the same ground with the same ideology.

The dogs themselves genuinely love the competition and athleticism of their sport—a love they feel even years after retirement. At the Abilene Greyhound Park, my retired dogs got to run on the racetrack one last time—down the frontstretch and into the first turn. After the mock race, a handler walked them over to me in the pens. They had looks on their faces that seemed to say, "Did you see us, Daddy? Huh? Huh? Did you see us?" That was a wonderful moment for me.

Conversely, one of the worst things I experienced while creating this book was standing next to a group of trainers when a dog took a spill on the first turn. There was a collective gasp, and I heard a trainer cry out the dog's pet name in a way that wrenched my soul. The animal was entirely uninjured, even finishing the race, but the trainer was deeply shaken. None of the other trainers laughed or made fun of her because they had all been there before. Another difficult moment for me was watching a trainer worry about the fate of a sick dog. He was leaning on a fence, overwhelmed with concern for his pup. This was a very large individual—a man you might expect to meet in a raucous bar somewhere. But there he was, hunched over, with two other old trainers comforting him. I could have taken a picture—and I wanted to—but I couldn't bring myself to intrude on the man's painful moment.

These people care deeply about their dogs. On Fourth of July, they are in the kennel buildings to comfort thunder-phobic dogs that are frightened by the loud fireworks, often climbing into the crates with the dogs. On Christmas Eve and Christmas Day, as on any other day, they are in the kennel buildings, scrubbing food bowls and sweeping floors. While visiting the racetracks, I saw a universal dedication far beyond even that in the pet world at large. While I was learning firsthand, individuals on the Internet were still talking about how all of the dogs are terribly mistreated. But I learned the truth. As a dog lover who had taken his first steps with Greyhounds two decades prior, it was a truth I admired and wanted to share with others. I continued to support Greyhounds and racing because I discovered that the world of Greyhound racing is made up of dog lovers who have made great strides in promoting adoption and have developed productive relationships with adoption organizations. Everything I saw is represented in this book, from beginning to finish and from coast to coast. It is the world of Greyhound racing and adoption, and it is as unique as it is incredible.

Introduction

The Greyhound has the eyes of a philosopher and the soul of an ancient hunter. So old is the breed that the origins and true meaning of its name have been lost to history. The word *grey* was corrupted from something—perhaps "to gaze" or "that which is great." Unfortunately, we may never know why the dogs were labeled *grey* hounds. What is certain is that the Greyhound has walked beside us from the beginning of recorded history and is a companion not just to individual humans but to humankind.

During the mid-nineteenth century, Americans imported Greyhounds to help control the spread of jackrabbits, which were destroying crops throughout the Midwest. Soon after the dogs' arrival, coursing clubs began to form, and in 1886 the American Coursing Board was founded as the first national coursing registry in the country. In October 1906, the National Coursing Association—renamed National Greyhound Association in 1973—was established using the registration records from the by-then-defunct American Coursing Board.

The actual sport of Greyhound racing as it is known today was the brainchild of Owen Patrick Smith, an inventor who spent years developing a practical mechanical lure system. In 1919, O. P. Smith opened his first racetrack in Emeryville, California, with a mechanical lure that weighed some 1,500 pounds. Known as the Blue Star Amusement Company, the racetrack lay on the outer fringes of Oakland and rarely drew a crowd of more than three hundred spectators.

In our technological age of highspeed this and drive-through that, the one thing that can still touch the human spirit like nothing else is the special bond between people and their dogs. Simplistic in nature, it is ancient and powerful.

Running lighter than air, Iowa-bred L's Main Event is just seconds away from earning his first win at Bluffs Run Casino. Roughly a year later, he matured into a grade-A racer at the Dubuque Greyhound Park in Dubuque, Iowa.

Without pari-mutuel wagering in place, the sole purpose of the racetrack was to exhibit the sights and sounds of Greyhounds in full flight, with profits generated entirely by gate receipts—a way of operating that would never be repeated by future racetracks. After the 1921 season meet, Smith's first and short-lived racetrack was understandably relegated to history.

In 1921, Smith opened four racetracks in Florida, Illinois, Kansas, and Oklahoma. The Mid Continent Park in Tulsa, Oklahoma, was the first financially successful operation. Incredibly, to find enough Greyhounds to actually race at the Mid Continent Park, Smith was forced to drive from one local farm to another in an effort to round up as many Greyhounds as he could.

For the small number of Greyhound owners and their canine athletes, life was anything but stationary during the 1920s. Most traveled across the country either on passenger trains or in their Tin Lizzies with luggage strapped to their roofs and a couple of dogs riding in their backseats. Owners, fascinated by the new sport, would drive thousands of miles over dusty or muddy country back roads to reach distant racetracks, some of which were only rumored to have opened. Such was the mindset during the 1920s, when most people were able to enjoy leisure, travel, and sport for the first time in American history.

With less than three dozen Greyhounds available to race at almost any given racetrack during the time, many races had only two dogs competing against each other—essentially a match race. Most Greyhounds raced at least twice a day, with the winners pitted against each other until one dog remained unbeaten. Sometimes as many as six dogs would take to the racetrack at once, being released from an early version of the starting box with doors that opened vertically.

Despite the initial scarcity of competitors, Greyhound racing began setting down firm roots in the country, which allowed it to survive not only the turbulence of the twenties but also the depredations of the Great Depression and the demands of World War II. In January of 1945, the director of War Mobilization and Reconversion closed both Greyhound and Thoroughbred racetracks throughout the country to save labor and critical materials for the war effort. The sport of Greyhound racing entered the 1950s as an established, albeit localized, spectator sport. In 1950, twenty-seven racetracks in seven states—as well as one in Tijuana, Mexico—hosted seasonal racing meets that lasted for several months each year.

During that same year, the Hartwell grading system was employed for the first time at the Cavalier Kennel Club, situated in Moyock, North Carolina. The grading system, named after its inventor, Paul Hartwell, assigns Greyhounds to a specific grade—A, B, C, D, and so on—that ensures a Greyhound with certain speed abilities will race against other Greyhounds of the same skill level and ensures fairness by giving each racer an equal number of starts. Although some racetracks have tweaked the procedures of the grading system, it remains in use today.

Throughout its storied history, the sport of Greyhound racing has evolved from a collection of dusty racetracks peppered over several states to a national industry that spends great resources on the care and welfare of its canine athletes. Welfare guidelines created by the National Greyhound Association cover nutrition, housing, kennel cleanliness, exercise, and health of Greyhounds. To enforce its welfare guidelines, the NGA sends unannounced inspectors to breeding farms annually.

From the onset of racing in 1919, owners began to employ the practice of selective breeding in an effort to create the fastest dog possible. As a result, the racing Greyhound slowly but surely morphed into something different from its canine forefathers and even from its contemporary American Kennel Club relatives bred for conformation.

The actual practice of selective breeding is an inexact science, as Greyhound breeders will freely admit. But as the old saying goes, "like tends to beget like." With nearly a century of selective breeding to improve attributes such as good health, athletic fortitude, confidence, and intelligence, the racing Greyhound known today is an extremely healthy breed and also a wonderful pet that has found its way into thousands of homes throughout the country.

The racing industry has formed numerous positive relationships with adoption organizations; with their combined efforts, the goal of a national 100 percent adoption rate is being

With a dark brindle coat—a color of wild dogs—Abby (Courtney Rush-PH, AP, TU) recreates the look of an ancient ancestor while lying in a shady Salem, Oregon, backyard. The brindle coat serves as camouflage and is a product of a gene passed on from Greyhound to Greyhound for thousands of years.

realized. Currently, out of around 26,000 Greyhounds registered each year, roughly 20,000 are adopted to private homes and another 4,250 are returned to breeding farms to either bring in the next generation or live out their lives as pets. Thanks to the efforts of adoption volunteers and support from the racing industry, the retired racing Greyhound is now accepted by the American public as one of the best house pets a family can own.

While the sport of Greyhound racing and the adoption of its canine athletes have established themselves in countries such as Australia, England, and Ireland, the concepts were born in the United States. The sport is as American as the Statue of Liberty, Cape Canaveral, the Alamo, the Rocky Mountains, or the Space Needle. Like these icons—regional yet still uniquely American—Greyhound racing and adoption is a part of our great country from coast to coast. The following chapters represent my journey and the areas to which I traveled, homes to some of the nation's great racetracks. I encourage readers to learn more about Greyhound racing and to seek out racetracks and adoption efforts in their areas.

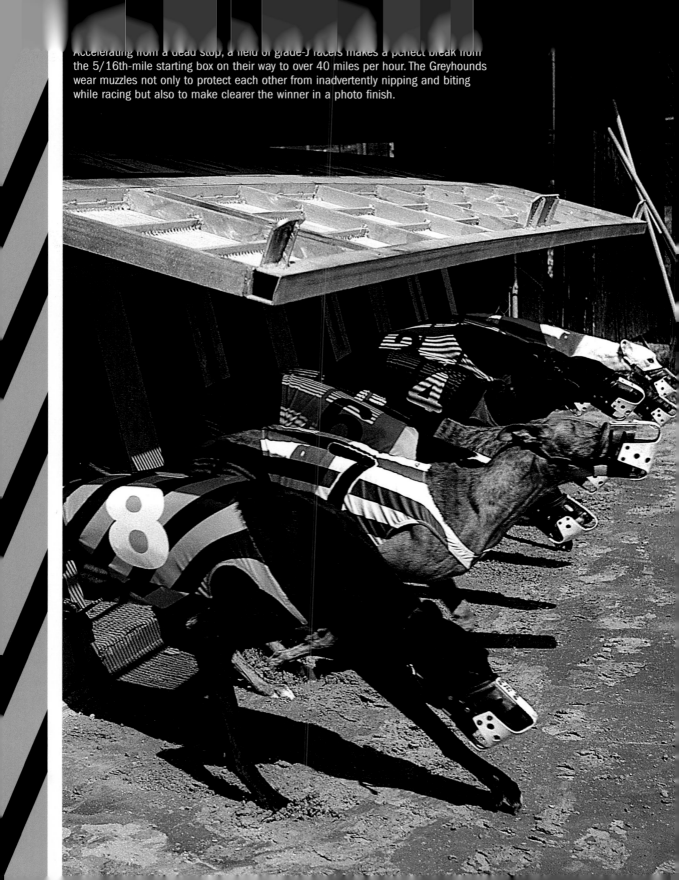

Accelerating from a dead stop, a field of grade-J racers makes a perfect break from the 5/16th-mile starting box on their way to over 40 miles per hour. The Greyhounds wear muzzles not only to protect each other from inadvertently nipping and biting while racing but also to make clearer the winner in a photo finish.

CHAPTER 1

NORTHEASTERN STYLE

From the short-lived Atlantic City Kennel Club of the Roaring Twenties to Massachusetts's iconic racetracks to the former Thoroughbred racetrack in Rhode Island reborn as the Lincoln Greyhound Park, Greyhound racing in the Northeast is a study in diversity. During the early 1930s, dozens of racetracks opened and then closed after a single seasonal meet of perhaps only a few months, never to open again, while Massachusetts's Wonderland and Raynham Parks, which opened in 1935 and 1940, respectively, flourished. In the 1970s, Rhode Island and Connecticut opened their own Greyhound racetracks. During the 1990s, video lottery machines were installed at some of the racetracks, turning them into racetrack/casino hybrids known as *racinos*. At the same time, adoption efforts for retired Greyhound racers became a priority for everyone involved with the sport.

With a rich history of Thoroughbred and Greyhound racing, Lincoln Park was a Rhode Island icon for more than half a century.

On July 7, 1923, Greyhound racing was thrust into mainstream politics when the Atlantic City Kennel Club opened its racetrack for its second annual meet. Unfortunately for the kennel club, New Jersey lawmakers at the time viewed gambling as a sign of human weakness and even a threat to social morality. Less than three weeks after the opening, on July 26, Atlantic City detectives raided the racetrack on the order of New Jersey Prosecutor Louis Repetto, who arrested the racetrack operators and closed down the premises. With the exception of limited racing during 1926, the Atlantic City Kennel Club would not see Greyhound racing again until 1933. A year later, racing ended for good at this location.

To the north in Massachusetts, Greyhound racing was faring much better during this time. In 1934, the same year in which racing was shut down in New Jersey, the Massachusetts Legislature legalized pari-mutuel wagering, thus paving the way for three state-sanctioned racetracks to open in 1935—Wonderland Park in Revere, the Crescent Kennel Club in Springfield, and the Bristol County Kennel Club (later renamed the Taunton Kennel Club) in Taunton. By 1940, the Crescent Kennel Club was out of business, replaced by Raynham Park in the city of Raynham.

It was at the Taunton Kennel Club in 1949 that the American Greyhound Derby was established. It was the first championship stake race open to any dog in the world; the winner, therefore, was titled World Champion. On September 10, 1950, the stake race was aired nationally on the National Broadcasting Company (NBC)—a first for the sport of Greyhound racing. (The Taunton Kennel Club hosted the American Greyhound Derby until 1985; thereafter, the stake was hosted by Rhode Island's Lincoln Greyhound Park.)

Massachusetts's Raynham Park, Wonderland Park, and the Taunton Kennel Club would remain the only Greyhound racetracks in the New England region until the early 1970s, when New Hampshire legalized Greyhound racing, allowing the Hinsdale and Seabrook Greyhound Parks to open. The Hinsdale Greyhound Park, originally built in 1958 as a seasonal harness racetrack, opened to Greyhound racing in 1972, making it a dual facility. (Harness racing at Hinsdale continued until the 1985 season, when local economics forced its discontinuance.) The Seabrook Greyhound Park opened the following year on July 2—amazingly, just three months after construction had begun at the racetrack facility. Unfortunately, Massachusetts voters took away the legalization of Greyhound racing in the state, forcing an end to the sport as of January 1, 2010.

The Plainfield Greyhound Park opened in 1976 in neighboring Connecticut; it would be another two decades before the state's second Greyhound racetrack, the Shoreline Star Greyhound Park, would open on November 1, 1995. Both racetracks in Connecticut would eventually suffer from dwindling attendance that would ultimately lead to their demise.

The Plainfield Greyhound Park closed its doors on May 14, 2005; the Shoreline Star Greyhound Park closed on May 29, 2006.

In Rhode Island, the Lincoln Greyhound Park (later renamed Lincoln Park, and then Twin River), located in the city of Lincoln, ran its inaugural Greyhound race on June 23, 1977. The first seasonal meet barely topped one hundred days, a far cry from its schedule of three hundred days per year seen in later years. The addition of broadcast video simulcast signals in 1991 allowed patrons to wager on races from different racetracks, thus broadening the patron base.

By the end of 1992, Greyhound and Thoroughbred racetracks in Rhode Island had been allowed to install video lottery machines, converting their respective facilities into racinos. On September 15, 1999, Lincoln Park was granted permission to add five hundred new video lottery machines—bringing its total to twelve hundred—despite Governor Lincoln Almond's request for an emergency injunction against the Rhode Island State Lottery Commission. By 2002, Lincoln Park boasted some seventeen hundred machines.

Tucked into roadside foliage, a solitary billboard offers a hint about some of the changes that have taken place there over the decades. Originally built in 1947 as a Thoroughbred racetrack known as Lincoln Downs, the facility closed its doors in 1976 only to be purchased and converted into a Greyhound racetrack the following year. Later, in 1992, gaming was introduced with the installation of video lottery terminals, forever transforming the racetrack into a racetrack/casino hybrid. Having dropped the name Lincoln Park after a major expansion, the facility is known today as Twin River. In August 2009, Twin River suspended live racing, but reopened with different kennel operators.

GREYHOUND ADOPTION IN New England

The Rhode Island Greyhound Owners Association (RIGOA) was conceived in 1980 to protect the interests of Greyhound racing in the Ocean State by lobbying in the capital. At the time, the state of Rhode Island was preparing to tax the racing kennels out of existence, and something had to be done to preserve the sport. Thus, the RIGOA was created and sanctioned by Lincoln Park, Rhode Island's sole Greyhound racetrack, to fight the tax case, later winning in court.

By 1990, the RIGOA had turned into a genuine lobbying force that was dealing with multiple legislative issues. Yet, at the same time, the association was morphing into something else altogether: a benevolent group serving the needs of retired racing Greyhounds as well as Rhode Island's underprivileged citizens.

In recent years, the RIGOA has donated around $100,000 annually to Greyhound adoption efforts, plus another $150,000 to local charities. The single biggest recipient of the RIGOA's benefaction is the Lincoln Greyhound Adoption Program, founded in late 1994 and later known as Twin River Greyhound Adoption. To get the organization started, the RIGOA paid for an adoption kennel in the secure Lincoln Park kennel compound, as well as a brand-new van to provide transportation. Electricity, telephone service, food for the retired racers, and even furniture expenses are also covered by the owners' association.

Summing up the relationship, adoption director June Bazar said, "Whatever we need, we get. Our kennel wouldn't be here if it wasn't for the RIGOA. All they care about is what's best for the dogs, and I love them like family." With their combined efforts, approximately two hundred retired racing Greyhounds were adopted through the Twin River Greyhound Adoption Program each year, allowing the racetrack to enjoy a 100 percent adoption rate while it was hosting live racing.

In Massachusetts, the Wonderland and Raynham Greyhound Parks worked in conjunction with one another to host an annual Greyhound Adoption Expo at their respective facilities in Revere and Raynham. The expos drew some 450 attendees, and the schedule of events included a mock race—called a "fun run"—for retired racing Greyhounds, an amateur racing demonstration, speakers, raffles, racetrack tours, and even weeklong gigs as helpers in a racing kennel as prizes for some lucky adoption representatives.

Hidden away in the quiet corner of northeastern Connecticut near Pomfret Center is a breeding farm that embodies New England charm. Fred Fulchino started the Regall Sports kennel in April 1997 after spending a good deal of his life working in Greyhound racing. Fred's career has taken him from the position of leadout at the Wonderland Greyhound Park in Revere, Massachusetts, to being the owner of the highly acclaimed racer EA's Itzaboy, captain of the 2003 All-American Team. With the assistance of two kennel helpers, Fred cares for eighty to one hundred Greyhounds at any one time.

In a moment of simple pleasure, four-year-old Capones Lil jumps for joy while Fred walks her around the breeding farm during a chilly September morning in 2003. Two years earlier, the brindled speedster won the $75,000 Great Greyhound Race at the Seabrook Greyhound Park.

A tub of kibble, ground beef, cooked macaroni, and powdered supplements is prepared for the pups, who have built up an appetite after running and playing throughout the day. Once the future racers have finished eating, their individual bowls are collected, washed, and neatly stacked, ready for the next meal—a ritual that takes place twice a day, every day, whether it be an average Monday or Christmas Day.

Full of curiosity, energy, and life, pups of different ages and bloodlines spend a sunny afternoon playing and acting downright silly. Fenced 250-foot-long sprint paths give the youngsters enough room to stretch their growing legs when the mood strikes. Their New England way of life is a good one.

Aiding first-time patrons and professional handicappers alike, the tote board at a racetrack displays pertinent information, such as time to post, odds, pools, results, and payoffs for each race.

Running for the sheer joy of running, an eleven-month-old pup—bred from sire Craigie Whistler and dam Mohican Topaz—kicks up a cloud of dust in his sprint path during an early morning romp. While Greyhounds are trained to refine their innate athletic aptitudes just like any other athlete is, they are not trained to run or be competitive—that comes naturally from eight thousand years of instinct.

Three-year-old Flying Kulwicke (number 5) is slowly losing her slim lead to Erupter (number 7), a slightly younger pup who crossed the wire just ahead of the steely-eyed black beauty. After a successful racing career, Flying Kulwicke eventually became a brood matron.

◀ With a matinee scheduled for 12:20 in the afternoon, a great deal of work needs to be done, starting at sunrise. The sounds of heavy machinery will beckon and the smell of diesel exhaust will begin to hang low in the New England morning air. A few minutes after sunrise, Tony Blinkhorn—a starter/maintenance manager for Lincoln Park—goes to work on the racetrack by first scraping up the top 6 inches of the sand-and-clay composite using a motor grader. This process allows the composite to absorb the water needed to create a safe running surface. After several passes around the racetrack, the upturned composite is broken up and redistributed. On the curves, the composite is graded toward the outside edge to keep the degree of banking within proper standards.

▲ Once the racetrack surface has been upturned, Tony trades in the motor grader for a tractor that pulls a heavy dragging apparatus, which levels the surface. After several times around the track, the dragging apparatus is removed. The tractor, however, continues to circle the racetrack to tamp down the surface. After numerous passes, the racetrack is ready to absorb the predetermined and specific amount of water. Before the first race begins, the chute area and escape turn will be raked by hand. Because of this careful preparation of the racetrack, racing injuries are kept to an incredible minimum.

Trainers and handlers from the D.Q. Williams kennel unload their fleet-footed racers one by one as other kennel operators arrive at the paddock building for the weigh-in procedure. Faith Keeper and Storm Mist, the two white and fawn Greyhounds, along with Time Warp Lily and Showtime, the two black Greyhounds, are all solid AA to B racers.

In hot pursuit of Rhody, Lincoln Park's mechanical lure, BF Elli (number 2) leads the way of grade-BB racers. At this point in the race, the three-year-old speedster is pulling away from the pack and preparing to round the first turn in perfect form. While BF Elli took the win in 37.36 seconds, JJ's Slick (number 5) and PS Wise Choice (number 6) both made solid efforts and finished in second and third place, respectively.

While holding onto a half-dozen leashes with one hand, kennel operators must attach brass tags onto each Greyhound's collar with the other. Each brass tag has the number of a race and post position to identify what race and position each dog runs. Because trainers are used to the routine, the procedure is completed in a surprisingly short time.

Leadouts walk CTW About Sissy (number 5), Kiowa Salvo Cade (number 3), CJ Big Brother (number 2), and Flying Hunter (number 6) during a post parade. The platform in the foreground is used as a stage to photograph the winners of championship stake races, such as the American Derby, Lincoln Inaugural, and All-Age Sprint Stake.

▧ Running a step and a breath behind Radiant Mantle* (number 8), Flying Hunter (number 6) holds behind the leader just feet from the first turn. At the far turn, the yellow-jacketed pup muscled his way into the lead, winning the grade-C race by two lengths. (The asterisk behind a Greyhound's name means that the dog was whelped overseas.)

▼ Two-year-old Pa's Brethren (number 5) holds off Just Believe (number 7) to take another grade-AA win for the Regall Sports kennel. By the end of 2004, Pa's Brethren had raced in a half-dozen stake races at Lincoln Park and the Hollywood Greyhound Track in Hollywood, Florida.

A field of grade-M racers, some of whom only have one or two starts to their credit, break from the starting box and race down the chute. Atisa (number 1) took the win by powering herself past the leaders on the backstretch. A few months later, Atisa was racing in grade J at the Gulf Greyhound Park in La Marque, Texas.

1650 FT.

 Leadouts move into position to leash up their assigned Greyhounds as the canine athletes enter the escape turn after a grade-A race. The curtain, hanging by chains at the right and out of view, serves as an important safety measure in case a Greyhound falls while negotiating the first turn. Quickly pulled across the racetrack in such a situation, the curtain will prevent a disoriented dog from running in the opposite direction and head-on into speeding traffic.

▲ Blink An Miss, a rare blue-colored Greyhound, is walked off the racetrack and into the cool-off area for a quick spray of water, a drink, and the inevitable urine test to check the dog's system for illegal stimulants after winning a grade-A race. After a seventeen-month stay at Lincoln Park, Blink An Miss will return to his home racetrack, the Wichita Greyhound Park in Wichita, Kansas.

The post-race routine might first appear to be a strange mess of people and dogs, but it is a remarkably fast and smooth operation. As leadouts remove the stretchvest-type racing jackets from each Greyhound, trainers are standing by, ready to take their respective racers for a cool-down with chilled water.

Blasting through the first turn, Clair Has Flair (number 7), Spinning Spell* (number 3), and French Follie (number 8) battle for the lead position. A second later, French Follie was bumped, taking her out of contention for the lead. Spinning Spell* went on to take the grade-A win with Storm Mist (number 5), barely visible, holding on for second place. The Irish import Spinning Spell* had previously raced at Dublin's Shelbourne Park as well as at the Limerick Greyhound Track.

The Twin River Adoption Program's kennel houses retired racers just the same as any given racing kennel—a practice commonly seen at adoption kennels throughout the country. To help maintain a sense of security for the retired racers while in their new surroundings, feeding and turnout times are the same as those in the racing kennels. Likewise, males and females are turned out in separate pens to prevent clandestine romances from taking place. Because of the strong working relationship between the RIGOA and the adoption organization, Lincoln Park (Twin River) enjoyed a 100 percent adoption rate.

Rhode Island Greyhound Owners Association vice president Dan Ryan and Lincoln Greyhound Adoption Program director June Bazar, along with June's nine-year-old retired racer China (China Bay–LI), take in the sunshine at Lincoln's Saylesville Park as children enjoy playground equipment purchased using a $26,000 grant from the RIGOA.

The biggest recipient of the RIGOA's benefaction was the Lincoln (Twin River) Greyhound Adoption Program, founded in late 1994. June Bazar, a Greyhound Pets of America volunteer who had started in Greyhound adoption some fifteen years prior, was asked to serve as director for the upstart organization. The RIGOA footed the bill for the construction of a new adoption kennel next to the kennel compound at Lincoln Park. Once the kennel building was finished, the RIGOA purchased stylish black leather furniture for the lobby.

Tailwind Force (number 6) challenges Roar Phantom (number 1, in red) for the lead position in a stunning display of athletic fortitude as the field of Greyhounds races down the front stretch during a grade-B performance. Tailwind Force powered her way to take the win, with Roar Phantom holding on for second place.

2 A VISION OF SUNSHINE

By any measure, Greyhound racing in the state of Florida is astonishing, spectacular, audacious... you get the picture. With close to a third of the nation's Greyhound racetracks located in the Sunshine State—including the world's oldest, Derby Lane—Florida is a bright spot for racing fans across the country. Its racing history stretches back to 1921. With so many racetracks in the state, it is not surprising that Florida also has numerous adoption organizations for retired Greyhound racers.

Towering high over Gandy Boulevard and 4th Street in St. Petersburg, a long-legged sign points the way to the oldest Greyhound racetrack in the world.

In 1921, just two years after Owen Patrick Smith opened the first Greyhound racetrack, located in Emeryville, California, the sport found its way to Florida with the opening of the Miami Kennel Club in Hialeah. This was one of the first racetracks to regularly run eight Greyhounds in a single race. The kennel club was also the first to host evening races under a row of floodlights. Although somewhat of an experiment at first, evening racing at the Hialeah racetrack proved to be a hit with local patrons, and other racetracks throughout the country soon adopted the practice. They did not, however, adopt Hialeah's grass racetrack surface, continuing to use sand and dirt instead.

Later, in 1925, the St. Petersburg Kennel Club and the nearby Tampa-based Six Mile Creek Kennel Club opened their respective racetracks. A group of local businessmen had built the St. Petersburg Kennel Club on timberland purchased from T. L. Weaver, an entrepreneur of the lumber trade. It was the first racetrack built by private interests other than those of O. P. Smith or his partner George Heintz. The St. Petersburg Kennel Club celebrated its grand inaugural race on January 3, 1925.

Shortly after the racetrack's grand opening, its owners ran into financial hardship and were no longer able to make payments on the initial land purchase. Possession of the property, along with its newly built racetrack, reverted back to T. L. Weaver. Instead of selling the racetrack or dismantling it, the lumber entrepreneur kept the facility—an ownership that has remained in the Weaver family ever since.

By 1930, five Greyhound racetracks were operating in Florida, including the Seminole Kennel Club in Jacksonville, the Biscayne Kennel Club in Miami, and the Miami Beach Kennel Club in nearby Miami Beach, along with the racetracks in St. Petersburg and Tampa. None of them was officially sanctioned by the state; nor were the competing Thoroughbred racetracks. To legalize pari-mutuel wagering in the state and thus prevent local sheriffs' departments from raiding and shutting down the racetracks, operators of both sports teamed up and pushed for a bill, which was signed into law in 1931.

On December 1, 1934, the Hollywood Kennel Club, located just south of Fort Lauderdale, held its grand inaugural race in subfreezing temperatures normally associated with places like North Dakota and Minnesota. A fledgling operation at first, the racetrack had an opening-night wagering handle (the collective amount wagered by patrons) of just under $14,000—a low figure by most standards. By 1940, however, the racetrack would be earning purses several times higher than realized in its founding days.

Less than a year after the inaugural race, on November 4, 1935, a Category One hurricane known as the "Yankee hurricane" made landfall near Miami Beach, causing significant damage to the Hollywood Kennel Club track, as well as to several kennel buildings nearby. At the racetrack, a nearly 100-foot-tall sign collapsed from the wind, roof sections were blown off the grandstand, and several windows were broken. The worst damage was inflicted on the kennel buildings, where some fifty dogs perished in the storm, leaving breeders and trainers heartbroken for years afterward.

World War II brought significant challenges to the sport of Greyhound racing in the Sunshine State; these included gas rationing, the departure of breeders and handlers to either fight in the war overseas or work in essential industries, and a general downturn in gambling, all of which had a strong negative effect on Greyhound racing. The Sarasota Kennel Club simply shut down for the duration of the war. The other Florida-based racetracks, including the St. Petersburg Kennel Club, struggled to stay open during the war. Out of necessity, they found innovative ways to bring patrons to the grandstands. Because of gas rationing, the only realistic means for people to reach the St. Petersburg racetrack was to ride a bus that, unfortunately, stopped a mile away from the facility. As a stopgap solution, racetrack officials rounded up a small fleet of open and covered wagons powered by horses or mules and even a pair of electric carts to transport patrons to and from the bus stop. Other than walking the long distance, these wagons were the only means of transportation to the racetrack. The effort not only helped the racetrack keep grandstand seats full, but more importantly, it also allowed patrons a means to enjoy themselves with a night of racing.

With World War II finally over, stabilization came to Florida's Greyhound racetracks as America transitioned out of its wartime economy. The Sarasota Kennel Club was reopened by

Topiary, the art of fashioning living plants into ornamental shapes, was a popular feature at the Tampa Greyhound Track. The racetrack opened for business in 1933 and operated until 2007. It was a strong community supporter; during 2003, it donated over $250,000 to local charities.

Jerry Collins for the 1945–1946 seasonal meet. In 1949, Derby Lane—formerly the St. Petersburg Kennel Club—demolished its original 1925-era wooden grandstand to make way for a new one constructed of steel and concrete. Almost three decades later, in 1977, the racetrack replaced its original veranda clubhouse with an additional enclosed grandstand.

Derby Lane continued to flourish in more recent decades. On March 4, 2006, it hosted the first annual Derby Lane Million—the richest stake race in Greyhound-racing history. A total of 9,343 patrons jammed their way into the racetrack to watch two-year-old Grey's Calibrator win by a nose. On March 3, 2007, two-year-old Flying Stanley won the second annual million-dollar stake by less than a half second. Today, fourteen Greyhound racetracks continue to operate in Florida—far more than in any other state.

GREYHOUND ADOPTION IN Florida

With more Greyhound racetracks than any other state, Florida understandably has a large number of adoption organizations working to find homes for retired racers—roughly thirty groups in all. The Greyhound Pets of America network includes seven chapters ranging from the Pensacola area, peppered throughout the panhandle, to West Palm Beach in the south.

At the Palm Beach Kennel Club, the racetrack works closely with volunteers of the Greyhound Pets of America's Florida/Southeast Coast chapter as well as with the Greyhound Adoption League. The Greyhound Adoption League has found homes for several hundred retired racers to date while the GPA's Florida/Southeast Coast chapter has seen several thousand Greyhounds pass through its adoption program during its long history. With so many Greyhounds ending their racing careers at Florida racetracks, many retired racers are transported out of the area to adoption organizations as far away as the Pacific Northwest.

▲ Greeting each other like the old friends that they are, Donna and eight-year-old Oneco Littlefoot share a moment inside an enclosed pen. During his rookie year, the 64-pound speedster won eleven races and was a finalist in the 1997 Gold Trophy Juvenile stake race at Derby Lane. After retirement, Oneco Littlefoot remained with Donna and Francesca to live out his life as a beloved pet.

▲ Best known for its two champion Greyhounds, Talentedmrripley and Cayman Went, the Bahama Mama breeding farm raised roughly sixty puppies each year—enough to fill a racing kennel—until shutting down its operations in 2006. The breeding farm, which was owned by Donna Moore and Francesca Field, was built near Ocala, Florida, from the ground up in 2002.

◀ When Sugar, who was never registered with a racing name, was three months old, her front leg was broken—probably from her mother's stepping on it—and had to be amputated. Instead of being put to sleep, Sugar was kept at the breeding farm as a pet. She is able to run at high speed with other Greyhounds and function normally in every regard. Sugar acts like any of her four-legged counterparts, even hogging a couch when it's time to relax.

▲ Six-month-old puppies whelped from Oshkosh Slammer and Libby's Star waste away the afternoon in their own private canine clubhouse at Suncoast kennels after a morning full of running and playing. On the wall in the background, a well-placed waterspout works similarly to a drinking fountain for pups wanting a cool drink.

Just down the road from Plant City, Florida, and situated in lush green surroundings is the aptly named Suncoast kennels, owned by Randy and Deneen Ward, who started the breeding farm in the summer of 1989. Of the 140 Greyhounds that call Suncoast home, thirty-five are retired racers being cared for until adoption organizations can take them.

Deneen makes her rounds with a box of large dog biscuits for all 140 Greyhounds—racing and retired alike—exhausting the entire box in less than fifteen minutes. After eating his treat, three-year-old retired racer Eeyore (Atascocita Quake–OR, SO) shows Deneen his appreciation by pressing his nose against hers while showing off his big smile. Eeyore's sweet affection is returned with a heartfelt kiss from Deneen.

from Stan's Boy Flyer and Maryville Ellie vie to be the next through the gate and into the sprint path at the Cahill and O'Conner breeding farm. Tim Cahill only allows two out at a time, however, to keep the frisky puppies out of trouble.

▲ Established in October 1992 near the small town of Ona, the Cahill and O'Conner breeding farm raises up to thirty puppies at a time. The king of the castle, however, is eight-year-old Fever (Kiowa Fever–PB), a retired racing Greyhound. Instead of being sent to an adoption organization following his retirement, Fever remained at the breeding farm as a pet.

◀ With the morning turnout completed and treats handed out, Deneen now has a kennel full of content and sleepy Greyhounds who will snooze away the afternoon. The

Sheathed in history and rich in tradition, Derby Lane—the oldest Greyhound racetrack in the world—has become a rock of ages for Greyhound racing fans. In 1925, patrons walking into the grandstand would have looked up to see automobile-size letters spelling out "St. Petersburg Kennel Club" in all capitals. Today, red neon lights get the job done.

The puppies kick up dust at the Cahill and O'Conner breeding farm as they race past their still-confined littermates, running for the love of running and because they are Greyhounds. Roughly a year later, these puppies were ready for maiden races at the Palm Beach Kennel Club.

▲ Stan's Boy Flyer (RIGHT) and his two-year-old son, Bud's Around, casually mingle around the water bucket during an afternoon turnout at the Cahill and O'Conner breeding farm. Stan's Boy Flyer enjoyed an extremely successful racing career at the Palm Beach Kennel Club, Tampa Greyhound Park, and Derby Lane. In that time, he came in first, second, or third in several stake races. Following in his papa's pawprints, Bud's Around has raced in several stake races himself.

Prior to each day of racing, Greyhounds pass through the paddock; there, the dogs are weighed, identified by the paddock judge, given brass tags listing what race and post position they will be in, and given racing jackets. With the large amount of currency wagered on each race, strict state-mandated regulations are enforced during the weigh-in procedure.

Getting dressed for his next race, Trix Morgan E is given the red racing jacket with number 1. Not as durable as the older, buttoned-up racing jackets, the Australian-made stretchvest-type jackets require special care when being put on or taken off a Greyhound.

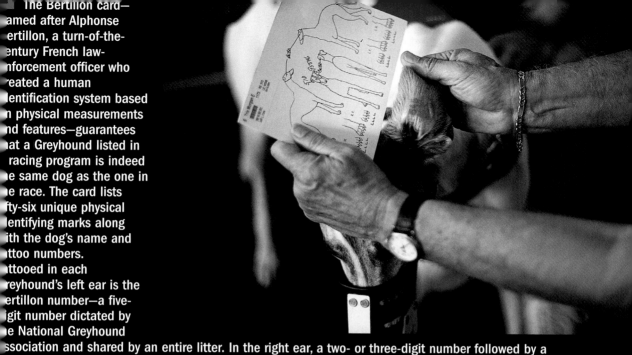

The Bertillon card—named after Alphonse Bertillon, a turn-of-the-century French law-enforcement officer who created a human identification system based on physical measurements and features—guarantees that a Greyhound listed in a racing program is indeed the same dog as the one in the race. The card lists fifty-six unique physical identifying marks along with the dog's name and tattoo numbers. Tattooed in each Greyhound's left ear is the Bertillon number—a five-digit number dictated by the National Greyhound Association and shared by an entire litter. In the right ear, a two- or three-digit number followed by a letter shows in what month and year the dog was whelped and in what order the dogs were tattooed. If a Greyhound was the first to be tattooed in a litter in October 2009, for example, the tattoo would read "109A." (The first three digits from "2009" are omitted.)

◀ Greyhounds are weighed on their race day by the clerk of scales on a calibrated scale. This can prove to be difficult when the racers are bouncing with anticipation.

▲ Sprinting down the front stretch at Derby Lane, WP's Willow (number 5) and Coca Bongo (number 3) run neck and neck for the lead during a grade-A race. Right behind the leaders, Mine Sweeper (number 7) and Nikki Di (number 1) battle for third place with Fuzzy's Cannon (number 6) holding on the inside.

◀ About a second later, Mine Sweeper holds the outside just as a hole opens up between the leaders, allowing Fuzzy's Cannon to make his move to the inside. As the field rounds the first turn, Fuzzy's Cannon keeps the inside all to himself as he runs away with another grade-A win by three lengths.

◄ Leadouts walk a field of grade-D racers around the first turn and onto the front stretch during a post parade. Wearing the number-8 racing jacket is 73-pound Rosebud Bob, who raced in the Derby Lane/Tampa Greyhound Park circuit for another year after this photo was taken before moving to the Shoreline Star Greyhound Park in Bridgeport, Connecticut.

▲ Overlooking the racetrack from the judges' stand, racing officials, including the presiding and associate judges, compare notes during the short lull between races. From their vantage point, the officials have an unobstructed view of the entire racetrack.

Having just circled a meticulously maintained infield with a field of grade-B racers, three-year-old RL Joshua is just moments away from earning his nineteenth career win.

▲ Sand from two leading Greyhounds is still airborne as Eyesa Can Too races to the finish during a grade-M performance. After getting jammed on the front stretch, the youngster found himself in last place as the field sprinted into the first turn. Showing absolute determination, he hugged the rail and made up enough ground to earn a very impressive third-place finish. Five days later, Eyesa Can Too won his first maiden race by two lengths, lifting him to grade D and launching a racing career that ultimately realized 182 starts.

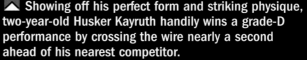 Showing off his perfect form and striking physique, two-year-old Husker Kayruth handily wins a grade-D performance by crossing the wire nearly a second ahead of his nearest competitor.

 In a blur of motion, WW Gravel Train (number 2, blue jacket) edges out the field for a grade-B win for the Wayne R. Ward kennel. The white and red brindled pup chased the mechanical lure in 185 races throughout his racing career, which included twenty-six wins.

At the Calabro Farm located just outside of Underwood, Iowa, Sue Calabro holds up a four-week-old puppy (Fortified Power–Cals Brindle One) who was named Cals Locomotion. After schooling, he went on to race at the Geneva Lakes Greyhound Track in Delevan, Wisconsin.

CHAPTER 3

CORN BELT REVIVAL

Greyhound racing had dubious beginnings in Iowa, deep in the nation's Corn Belt. Officials in the Hawkeye State squashed early efforts to establish the sport so completely that it was not until the 1980s that Greyhound racing was legalized and took hold. Nearly forty-two years prior to the passing of the Pari-Mutuel Wagering Act by the Iowa Legislature, a little-known yet highly controversial racetrack had made a mark in the Corn Belt. In early 1941, organized crime boss Meyer Lansky came to Council Bluffs with plans to build a Greyhound racetrack—even though pari-mutuel wagering was illegal in Iowa at the time. Lansky carried a degree of influence with the governor, who saw Greyhound racing as a potential source of revenue; with that, the Dodge Park Kennel Club was born.

Sitting on a little over 72 acres, Bluffs Run Casino employs over eight hundred people and attracts thousands of patrons each year who hope to beat the odds. Unlike seasonal racetracks that host live racing only during certain months each year, the racing at Bluffs Run Casino is a continuous running affair.

To sidestep the pari-mutuel law, a patron would buy a $2 or $5 "purchase option" for one or more Greyhounds running in a race. Options were for win, show, or place—just as in pari-mutuel wagering. If a Greyhound finished in the top three, the value of the dog was increased accordingly and the purchase option was then resold back to the racetrack for a profit. As far as Lansky and the governor were concerned, all races were considered "exhibitions."

With legalities taken care of, at least on the surface, a $50,000 wooden grandstand and racetrack were built on land owned by the Council Bluffs Park Commission. Greyhounds took to the racetrack for the very first time on July 11, 1941, in front of a crowd of forty-five hundred patrons. Total attendance for the fifty-six-night meet nearly reached 150 thousand. The 1942 meet opened on July 5, followed by sixty nights of racing. The following year saw an eighty-six-night meet that opened on May 2.

As quickly as the racetrack sprang up, so it died. The planned 1944 meet was stifled by a newly elected city mayor who took a stand against the kennel club. Two years later, with yet another city mayor in office, a 1946 meet was planned to open on July 6. The racetrack was, however, kept closed by state officials, leaving the sport to languish in Iowa for the next four decades.

Beginning in January 1980, a mild seven-month-long recession bogged down the American economy. This was followed by another recession, much more severe than the first, lasting from July 1981 to November 1982. The economic downturn caused by the so-called "double-dip" recession hit the state of Iowa with sobering fury. By 1982, unemployment reached a level not seen since the Great Depression. Manufacturing production dropped by 20 percent and the agricultural situation was just as dire.

In Council Bluffs, this was old news. They had been experiencing hard times long before the double-dip recession took hold. Earlier, in the 1970s, some four thousand local jobs were lost due to downsizing of the railroad, the primary employer of the community. With little hope of economic growth, the city's self-image plummeted.

Faced with revenue shortfalls and a bleak outlook, Iowa politicians began to explore new ways to improve the local economy. As a result, Iowa Legislature passed the Pari-Mutuel Wagering Act in May 1983. Of the five Greyhound racetracks proposed, the Iowa Racing and Gaming Commission ultimately granted operation licenses to three: the Dubuque Greyhound Park in Dubuque, the Waterloo Greyhound Park in Waterloo, and the Bluffs Run Greyhound Park in Council Bluffs. Greyhound racing had finally returned to the Hawkeye State. Far removed from the vagabond years of wooden grandstands and questionable legalities, this time the dogs came to stay.

In Dubuque, a community still in the grip of high unemployment, 5,750 residents applied for the three hundred jobs offered by the new racetrack. After a great deal of anticipation and local fanfare, the city-owned Dubuque Greyhound Park opened its $10.1-million racetrack on June 1, 1985. Along with several state officials, 4,249 patrons were on hand as MB's Polo, a pup from the Nova kennel, won the first official Greyhound race in Iowa. At $212,713, the first night's wagering handle was somewhat below the $300,000 estimated by racetrack developers. But on November 17, when the Dubuque Greyhound Park concluded its first season, 5,079 patrons wagered a record-high $594,271.

On October 15, 1986, the Waterloo Greyhound Park celebrated its grand opening, becoming Iowa's third Greyhound racetrack. The smallest of the three racetracks in both size and cost, the $6.2-million facility was financed using $3.9 million in industrial development bonds, a $1-million loan from the city of Waterloo, and $875,000 in private loans. At the conclusion of the first season, patrons had wagered $6.8 million at the racetrack.

A wild display of light from the design of man and nature exists for a brief moment as the sun rises over Bluffs Run Casino during a crisp autumn morning in 2003. The racetrack began operations in February 1986 after being granted a conditional three-year license by the Iowa Racing and Gaming Commission. The casino was added later in March 1995.

On February 27, 1986, Greyhound racing made a spectacular return to Council Bluffs as 6,100 patrons attended Bluffs Run Greyhound Park's inaugural race. Despite the 30-degree temperature, the grand opening caused multiple traffic jams on Interstates 80 and 29 as Iowans flocked to the $18-million racetrack in hopes of being a part of the festivities. Many were turned away.

In contrast, the Waterloo Greyhound Park declared Chapter 13 bankruptcy in December 1993, ultimately closing its doors on July 13, 1996. The two remaining racetracks were thereafter transformed with the introduction of slot machines and prospered as racinos into the twenty-first century.

Running wild with more than eight thousand years of instinct raging through him, two-year-old Barts Kobe is a study of fury and grace. While fast on the straightaway, the pup has a great deal of trouble negotiating the turns and consistently runs wide, allowing the slower dogs to pull ahead. No matter, the gamely racer usually finishes strong and crosses the wire in the top three.

◀ In the sweltering heat and high humidity of an early September afternoon, Donna Lovely cleans turnout pens at her Pacific Junction, Iowa, breeding farm. Besides raising pups, Donna also maintains an adoption kennel for the Bluffs Run Greyhound Adoption Program.

▶ Three-month-old puppies from two different litters (Flying Saturn–TNT Star Wars and Bustinout Isabel–Scott Free) jostle for Donna's full attention. The puppy in her arms was eventually named Ogalalla Breeze. After a brief racing career at Wisconsin's Geneva Lakes Greyhound Park, she was sent to Team Greyhound Adoption of Ohio.

◀ Having a good time, pups of different ages and parentage make some noise to rile up their canine companions in a neighboring pen. Within minutes, most of the Greyhounds were howling at the top of their lungs. Iowa may be corn country, but Pacific Junction belongs to the dogs.

59

▲ The five-acre Greenview Farm, a breeding farm situated near the town of Treynor, is owned by Jeff Gubbels and his wife, Stacy, both of whom are trainers at Bluffs Run Casino. Dozens of Greyhounds, including a few retired racers kept as pets, call the farm home. Needing to unleash their passion for running, the youngsters are allowed out of the runs for an afternoon romp. After several minutes, the pups' antics finally caught the attention of five-year-old retired racer Lefty (CD Multicolor–DQ, BR). The four dogs ran along the fence line for more than ten minutes before Lefty gave up and retreated to a shady area for a nap.

After playing outside with their littermates, these high-energy puppies finally yield to their fatigue and nap away the rest of the afternoon.

An eight-week-old puppy (Traveling T-Gable Dodge) is hunched motionless, carefully studying his prey like a ferocious lion deep in the Serengeti. The prey—a bright yellow and black grasshopper—finally made a break for it and escaped into the tall grass.

◀ Wearing his game face, three-year-old Ohpa's Hermes stands ready just moments before the start of a grade-B race. Greyhounds that draw the number-one box at Bluffs Run Casino enjoy a far better chance of winning than any other position. Of the Greyhounds that won their races in 2004, 21 percent wore the red jacket compared with the next highest percentage, 13 percent, in the number-two box.

▶ After making a perfect break from the starting box, eight Greyhounds sprint down the chute and onto the racetrack for a grade-D performance. Wearing the green jacket (number 4), Byline Everready led the field from the beginning and won the race by one-and-a-half lengths. The pup tallied up 123 starts and fifteen wins during his three-year-long racing career.

▲ Leadouts walk a field of grade-TD racers onto the racetrack for a feature in which all competitors are Iowa-bred. For a Greyhound to qualify for Iowa-bred status, the dog has to be whelped in the state and raised for his first six months in Iowa by an owner that has been a state resident for at least two years prior to the whelping date. After six months, an Iowa-bred Greyhound can be sold or leased to another person without losing his status. Those who race Iowa-bred Greyhounds in the Hawkeye State qualify for larger commissions, paid by the Iowa Greyhound Association, if their racers win.

A field of grade-C racers led by three-year-old Alvin Macbarker (number 8) enters the first turn while running just feet away from the inside rail. For a brief time, the rail was painted brown to better match the color scheme of Bluffs Run Casino. However, the brown paint was short-lived when it was deemed potentially hazardous to the Greyhounds racing past it. The rail was then repainted with a coat of high-profile, bright white enamel.

◀ Throttling down from 40 miles per hour, Calm Down (number 4), D's Pride N Joy (number 7), and Koko Expressway (number 2) coast into the escape turn moments after completing a grade-D race. Unlike D's Pride N Joy and Koko Expressway, two dogs who raced only at Bluffs Run Casino, Calm Down eventually moved south to the Phoenix Greyhound Park, where he raced in grades AA, A, and B for several years.

▶ With eyes trained squarely on Lucky, the mechanical lure, Limitless (number 8), My CJ Savage (number 7), and KL's Curtis (number 2) lead a field of grade-A racers past the first turn marker. Limitless raced for another two years, enjoying a lengthy career before finally retiring in October 2005.

▲ Shape and shadow combine in a mesmerizing profile of two-year-old Jr's Ben. The pup began his racing career in November 2002, reaching grade A in just eight starts. He nearly broke the thirty-second barrier for a 503-meter race shortly afterward—a feat few Greyhounds racing at Bluffs Run Casino ever achieve. Making a business of winning, the brindled speedster earned his twentieth victory by holding on to an early lead in the race pictured here. Roughly a year later, Jr's Ben moved 1,300 miles away to compete at the Orange Park Kennel Club in Jacksonville, Florida, where he

◀ Two-year-old Daddy Brian jets alongside competing canine athletes during a grade-C performance. His name proved to be self-fulfilling prophecy as, after retiring in August 2005, Daddy Brian moved on to become a stud dog and fathered forty-four offspring in all.

▶ Three-year-old PB's Simon Sez is escorted off the racetrack along with his racing companions moments after a grade-A performance. Prior to coming to Bluffs Run Casino, he was a Colorado hotshot, running in grades A and AA at Mile High and Cloverleaf Greyhound Parks.

▲ A few steps over from where their jackets are removed, the dogs are given a spray of cold water to prevent overheating. Whether in rain, snow, or heat, care is given to protect the Greyhounds from outdoor conditions that can be detrimental to their well-being.

 In an environment where things move fast, the Greyhounds are stripped of their racing jackets and returned to their respective trainers within minutes—perhaps seconds—of being walked off the racetrack by leadouts. Given the amount of energy each dog just spent in racing one another, they are in need of refreshment.

◀ Having just finished fifth in a grade-TC Iowa-Bred Feature race, three-year-old Cals Super Shane is walked from the racetrack to the nearby kennel compound. The kennel compound, which is kept under tight security, is home to fifteen racing kennels that collectively house hundreds of Greyhounds.

▷ Looking somewhat like recess at an elementary school, a kennel's worth of Greyhounds soaks up the September sunshine during a midday turnout. While the pups relieve themselves, mingle, sniff, and simply relax with other racers, trainers—along with their assistants—busily clean soiled areas and replenish crates with new shredded newspaper.

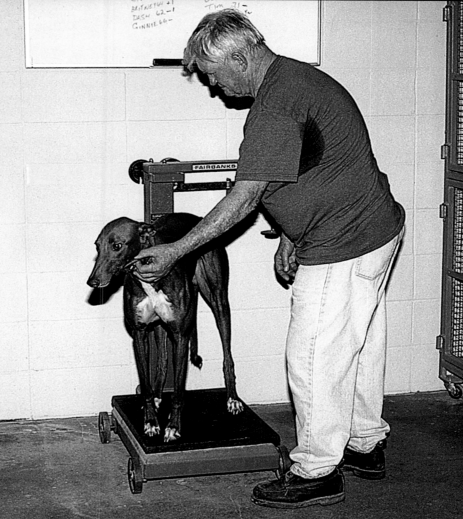

▷ Longtime trainer Don Conatser weighs 80-pound Bartselwoodblues on a scale in his kennel. There's no doubt that much hard work and many long hours go into running a racing kennel and properly caring for so many Greyhounds. An average day for Don can begin at 5 a.m. and last until 11 p.m. Because dogs need to be cared for, fed, and turned out every day, the routine happens 365 days a year—rain or shine. After bidding goodnight to his pups, Don is ready for a hearty dinner with a few trainers from competing kennels at Bluffs Run Casino's legendary steakhouse. "At the end of the day, it's all about the dogs," says Don. "That's why I'm here."

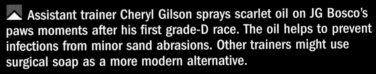 Assistant trainer Cheryl Gilson sprays scarlet oil on JG Bosco's paws moments after his first grade-D race. The oil helps to prevent infections from minor sand abrasions. Other trainers might use surgical soap as a more modern alternative.

The day before this picure was taken, three-year-old Rose (Bas Bleu Brown–PU, WS) crossed the wire for the final time during an evening race—a grade-E affair in which she finished sixth.

CHAPTER 4

KANSAN KALEIDOSCOPE

T he state of Kansas is where it all began for the breeding and raising of Greyhounds in the United States. Around the time that Kansas was granted its statehood, in 1861, local farmers began importing the dogs from Europe as a way to help control the ever-expanding jackrabbit population that was destroying valuable crops. By the late nineteenth century, Greyhounds had become a common sight in Kansas as well as in the neighboring states of Nebraska and Oklahoma.

Prior to the turn of the twentieth century, the sport of *coursing*—in which a pair of Greyhounds gives chase to a live rabbit within an enclosed field—had been a

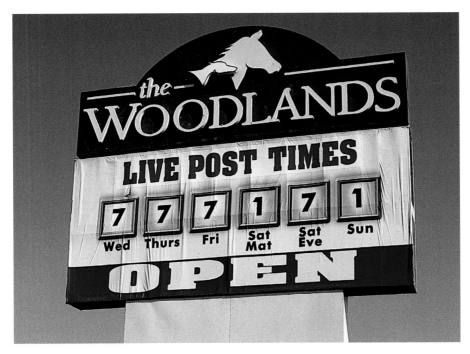

Towering high above Interstate 435, a few miles north of Kansas City, a stylish billboard shows post times for the dual racing facility.

popular pastime for the entertainment-starved locals. The exact origins of coursing in the Midwest have been lost to history; however, it probably started with competitive farmers bragging to one another about the speed, agility, athleticism, and intelligence of their prized Greyhounds. The first regulated coursing event in the United States took place in Cheyenne Bottoms, Kansas, in 1886.

Although Kansas had been home to numerous Greyhound breeding farms since the turn of the century and to the National Coursing Association since 1944 (it was renamed the National Greyhound Association in 1973), the state would not legalize pari-mutuel wagering until the late 1980s. Anthony Downs, which opened in Anthony in 1904 and was home to the county fair, ran Greyhound races as exhibitions only. In 1987, the state legislature finally passed the Kansas Pari-Mutuel Racing Act, opening the door to Greyhound and Thoroughbred racing in the state.

Greyhound racing in the Sunflower State officially launched on September 7, 1989, at the Wichita Greyhound Park; a black-and-white tuxedo pup named Abilene George won the Maiden Debut—the first pari-mutuel Greyhound race in the state. The first weekend drew 6,842 racing fans and curious locals to the $14-million racetrack.

Opening just one week after the Wichita Greyhound Park, the Woodlands Racetrack held its first race on September 14 after nearly a year of construction and at a cost of $68 million. The Woodlands Racetrack, located in the northwest corner of Kansas City, featured a separate Thoroughbred racetrack that, along with the Greyhound grandstand and kennels, took up 400 acres. In 1993, Anthony Downs allowed legalized pari-mutuel wagering for the first time.

A third and short-lived racetrack, the Camptown Greyhound Park, opened on May 17, 1995, near Pittsburg, Kansas. On November 5—less than six months after its grand debut—the $14-million racetrack suspended racing to avoid bankruptcy. Following a special meeting, the Kansas Racing Commission allowed the Camptown Greyhound Park to cancel its remaining 1995 meet, much to the disappointment of kennel operators and local racing fans.

Dealing with financial troubles of its own, the Woodlands Racetrack filed for bankruptcy protection on May 17, 1996. With the Camptown Greyhound Park having closed its doors the previous year and the Wichita Greyhound Park having cut back to save funds, the future of live Greyhound racing in Kansas seemed uncertain at best. However, despite a debt of more than $28 million, the Woodlands Racetrack remained open.

Over the next two years, the Woodlands Racetrack found itself in an entanglement of offers, proposals, legal issues, votes, hearings, rejections, and delays. Following two failed reorganization plans, the racetrack was finally liquidated. On December 16, 1998, ownership passed to construction and gambling mogul William M. Grace. In January 2000, annual revenue from betting rose at the Woodlands Racetrack for the first time in its decade-long history.

On June 9, 2000, the Camptown Greyhound Park, which had been shut down for five years, reopened under a new owner. The racetrack had a promising second start, and officials hoped that it would remain financially viable until slot machines were legalized in Kansas, allowing the racetrack to become a racino. Alas, Camptown Greyhound Park could not hold out; it closed for the second time on November 14, 2000, just seventy-four days after its reopening.

On May 4, 2003, a powerful F-4 tornado struck, nearly destroying the Woodlands Racetrack while racing was underway. The tornado passed through the parking lot and across the vacant Thoroughbred racetrack, just missing the grandstand and Greyhound kennels. No injuries were reported; however, electricity was lost after the storm, and the remaining four races had to be cancelled. Later in the month, the Woodlands Racetrack donated to the Salvation Army $3,200—funds received from network news corporations that had bought copies of the racetrack's surveillance tape showing the tornado.

One-year-old pups chase the mechanical lure on Herb "Dutch" Koerner's schooling racetrack. This is known as a rope track because the lure is tied to an actual rope that is guided around the racetrack by flanged wheels and propelled by a gasoline engine.

The following year, Anthony Downs celebrated its one-hundredth anniversary with the first race of its 2004 schedule. Probably the most unique operation in the sport of Greyhound racing, Anthony Downs is a pari-mutuel racetrack located on fairgrounds. It features both Greyhound and Thoroughbred racing, with the smaller Greyhound racetrack situated inside the Thoroughbred infield. Unlike most racing schedules that last for part or half of a year, the Anthony Downs meet is a six-day affair that takes place each July. A reflection of Greyhound racing during its earliest years, the Anthony Downs open-air grandstand, which was constructed during Theodore Roosevelt's presidential term, remains in use today. In addition, the small judges' stand is on the infield, as were those built in decades past. Today, most judges' stands are located above the grandstand.

By 2008, both the Woodlands Racetrack and the Wichita Greyhound Park closed their facilities due to taxation issues with the State of Kansas and the inability to legally install slot machines at their respective facilities. While one or both may reopen in the future, for the time being, Anthony Downs remains as the last racetrack in Kansas.

With little body fat and even less hair, Saidy Lou (Village Donna–MU) must wear a waterproof jacket to protect her from the chilly elements—in this case, a cold drizzle. In areas with severe weather, such as the Midwest, a thickly lined and waterproof jacket is a necessity for a Greyhound.

▲ Starlets in the making, four rambunctious eight- and nine-month-old pups make their voices heard during an afternoon romp. After schooling, the red-and-brindle pups (Braddy–Greys Shootnstar) moved to the Wheeling Island and Derby Lane racetracks, while their playmates—white-and-brindle pups (Molotov–Greys Shininstar)—raced at the Tri-State Greyhound Park near Charleston, West Virginia.

▶ With over 350 sires, dams, and puppies living on-site, Greymeadow kennels ranks among the largest breeding farms in the country. Greymeadow is located near Abilene and has produced some of the fastest Greyhounds in the sport. Co-owner Mary Butler, who is cradling a pair of twenty-day-old puppies (Flying Penske–Greys Witch Hunt) during a short break in the daily activity, has proven herself an adept administrator of the large breeding farm.

After having raced at Florida's Biscayne, Derby Lane, and Tampa Greyhound Parks, Greys Shininstar came to stay at Greymeadow as a brood matron. After her long career, the mother-to-many is shown caring for her sixth and final litter four days after they were whelped. She remains with her puppies for up to five weeks in a whelping box measuring roughly 5 feet by 6 feet. With an access door leading to an outdoor pen, Mom can come and go as she pleases. Until the puppies are ready to explore their outdoor pen, they will remain inside the climate-controlled kennel building.

◀ Although walkers are not found at many breeding farms, this one has been in service for over three decades. It is an essential part of Dutch's operation—especially for a Greyhound recovering from a past injury. The walker allows an injured dog to heal faster and stronger.

▲ Herb "Dutch" Koerner checks up on a litter of five-week-old puppies (WW Timewarp–Greys Headstand) at his breeding farm in Hays, Kansas. Dutch, a longtime breeder and past president of the National Greyhound Association, was inducted into the Greyhound Hall of Fame in 2001.

▲ Rotating at a steady 4 miles per hour, a mechanical walker lightly exercises brood matrons and Greyhounds needing either a gentle workout or recovery from past injuries. Brood matrons will be walked for up to an hour at least twice a week.

▲ Standing on an elevated platform complete with an instrument panel, Dutch controls the drag lure using a circular rope threaded between a pair of tires—one of which is powered by a six-cylinder engine salvaged out of a 1970 Mercury Comet.

◄ Before pups take to the schooling racetrack, they begin their training on a quarter-mile-long sprint path—first sprinting, then chasing a drag lure. Each pup will chase the drag lure eight to ten times, two or three times a week. Feeling a rippling intensity in the moment of releasing the dogs, kennel hand Jim Walt hand-slips a pair of pups who accelerate away with an ultra-smooth whoosh sound. During an hour-long session, each of thirty dogs takes a turn.

▲ Once they are deemed ready for the actual racetrack, pups at Dutch's breeding farm finally graduate to the schooling track. First racing in pairs and chasing a training-type lure—one that dangles from a rope—the pups eventually move on to race four at a time with the same kind of lure used at pari-mutuel racetracks.

▶ To keep Greyhounds' cuticles free of sand, thus preventing possible inflammation, each pup has his paws washed out with running water after racing; they will experience this procedure at any racetrack.

▶ The Woodlands Racetrack, located on the northwest fringe of Kansas City, Kansas, ranked as one of the most elegant Greyhound facilities in the country. The 400-acre complex featured forty-eight separate buildings to support its Greyhound racetrack, as well as a totally separate Thoroughbred racetrack located on the other side of a massive parking lot.

▲ Kansas-bred Crystal Lord (number 6) walks next to his leadout as they leave the paddock moments before a grade-M race—the pup's sixth career race at the racetrack. Crystal Lord went on to race in sixteen more races, peaking in grade C. Leadouts carefully avoid the freshly manicured racing surface, walking on the outermost edge of the racetrack during a post parade.

Grade-CT racers break from the starting box under a traditional broadside banner. GNC Lady Nicole (number 4) led throughout most of the race and crossed the wire in first place by a nose. The T in grade CT designates a mixed-grade race, such as C and D. The letter before the T indicates the highest grade allowed in the race.

Zoom Esther (number 7) holds next to the rail as N's Tan Man (number 1) and M's Crazy Legs (number 8) crowd him on the first turn. The rest of the field is out of the picture, trailing behind the leaders. Greyhounds are taught to run next to the rail, thus traveling a shorter distance than those on the outside and allowing for a better finish. Although N's Tan Man challenged for the lead on the final stretch, Zoom Esther held off her racing competitor

◀ Bursting into the sunlight at over 40 miles per hour, Kansas-bred GNC Just A Dog (number 3) leads the way as the eight Greyhounds sprint into the first turn. Crystal Lord (number 6) is hot on his tail and, despite bumping into another dog late in the race, took the win by a length and a half.

▲ PS Crystal Jazz (number 7) and Kansas Key (number 8) drive after the lure in a closely matched grade-D race. By this time in the race, PS Crystal Jaaz has established clear control, winning by three lengths.

▲ Winfra Silky (number 4), Primco Elm (number 1), and ICU Grady (number 2) blast through the first turn during a hotly contested grade-M performance. Three months later, Winfra Silky was racing at the Plainfield Greyhound Park in Plainfield, Connecticut; Primco Elm was at the Apache Greyhound Park in Apache Junction, Arizona; and ICU Grady was at the Naples–Ft. Myers Greyhound Track in Bonita Springs, Florida.

From the Greyhounds' point of view, the race ends at the escape, not at the actual finish line. This field of grade-D racers tries to bite and nip at the lure in the moments before the assigned leadouts remove the dogs from the racetrack. Just like at training tracks, muzzles protect the dogs' teeth while they try to bite the lure.

Ann Waitley, a longtime fixture at the racetrack, got her start in 1991 as the program manager. After being laid off during a general cutback three years later, Ann found employment as an assistant trainer, working in different racing kennels. Finally moving into the adoption world, she became the director of Pups Without Partners. This adoption organization, which was located within the kennel compound, was supported and financed by the Woodlands Racetrack prior to its closing on August 24, 2008. Today, Pups Without Partners has teamed up with another adoption organization, Kansas City REGAP (Retired Greyhounds as Pets), to continue finding homes for retired racers.

▲ Inside the Pups Without Patners adoption kennel, potential adopters meet and mingle with the Greyhounds to determine whether the dogs are a good fit for them—and vice versa, as not everyone qualifies to adopt a retired racer. As part of the adoption process, people who are new to the Greyhound are asked to read up on the breed to learn as much as possible about their new family members.

▲ During the home visit, adoption volunteers check for anything that can be potentially hazardous to a retired racer and advise on preventative measures. A fenced yard is generally the first requirement on the list. Some adoption organizations will refuse people who do not have fencing around their property; others require fencing higher than 4 feet. Without the protection of a fence, adopters must always walk their retired racers on a leash when the dogs need to relieve themselves or need exercise. Additionally, backyard landscaping is a common hobby for many homeowners, and tightly stretched support ropes are sometimes used to prop up small trees. Although these aids seem innocent to a potential adopter, a stretched rope is sometimes the cause of a broken leg or worse for a retired racing Greyhound with speed left to burn.

▶ Having been screened and ready to adopt a Greyhound, individuals return to the adoption kennel to select one or more retired racers. People often choose a Greyhound for his personality and, sometimes, a bond develops right there in the turnout pen. Walking out of the adoption kennel and into a new way of life—for both the adopter and adoptee—is an exciting experience, and one not soon forgotten. Many people are so impressed with the dogs that they return to adopt a second or third.

91

With eyes piercing the Kansas summer sky, Greyhound statues guard the entrance to the National Greyhound Association. For any Greyhound aficionado—anywhere in the world—to come to Abilene, even if it is for the very first time, is to come home.

▲ The National Coursing Association established the Greyhound Hall of Fame in 1963 to preserve and applaud the memories of those who built the sport into a national pastime and, as such, a three-pillar monument was erected on the NCA grounds as part of the original Hall of Fame. In recent years, the monument has become a gathering place for adoption volunteers and adopters during the annual Greyhound America event organized by Race the Wind Adoption. This is a gathering of adoption representatives, adopters, and their retired racers, along with breeders, trainers, racetrack operators, and National Greyhound Association employees, in which all come together and enjoy each other's company as dog lovers.

▲ A plaque on the center pillar explains why the Greyhound Hall of Fame came into being.

▲ Inside the NGA offices, registrations are issued for all racing Greyhounds in the United States. At times, the registration information also benefits retired racing Greyhounds. When a call comes in about a lost retired racer, employees do whatever they can to provide ear tattoo numbers to aid the search, even if the dog has not raced in several years.

97

The 2004 NGA spring meet is well underway as Go Bon Sometouch (number 5) waits with other pups moments before the start of race 19, the Redmoon Clyde and D.Q. Williams Stake. At auction the following day, Go Bon Sometouch sold for $2,000. One month later, the white-and-brindle pup was racing at the Jacksonville Kennel Club.

◄ In hot pursuit of Buddy, the mechanical lure, HK's Sky Rocket (number 4) blasts through the first turn with Kaycar Amy* (number 5) and KB's Royal Flush (number 7) not far behind. The green-jacketed, Texas-bred pup went on to easily win race 31, the Anicare Stake. After a long racing career at the Wheeling Island and Palm Beach racetracks in West Virginia and Florida, respectively, HK's Skyrocket was adopted as a pet by volunteers of Elite Greyhound Adoptions.

▶ Like proud parents at a high school football game, breeders and handlers watch their pups blast through the first turn during race 38, the Symbioum Farms Stake. Among the spectators is sixteen-month-old Flying Crusader, a pup who broke his maiden at the Gulf Greyhound Park in La Marque, Texas.

▲ Two 15-month-old pups, Capturethemoment (number 2) and Roscoepcoltrane (number 5) make race 46, the Clear the Way Stake, a close one as they sprint toward the backstretch. Kay Cari K Mart, out of the picture, took the win by nosing out Capturethemoment at the wire. Like many other pups, Kay Cari K Mart sold for $20,000 the next day.

◀ Pools of water offer a stark reminder of the torrential rains that fell earlier in the morning as Craigie Director (number 5) powers through the first turn with Matt's CJ (number 2) hanging on in second place during race 8, the Palm Beach Kennel Association Stake.

▼ Shortly after the final race, a brood-stock auction gets underway at the Abilene fairgrounds. Roughly halfway into the auction, four-year-old Chasmo's Dixie, a former racer from Lincoln Park who raced consistently in grades A and AA, is walked in front of a crowd of bidders and spectators. The final bid for the Greyhound is $5,250. The highest price paid for a brood bitch during the auction was $10,250.

▲ Built to celebrate the heritage of Greyhound racing, the Greyhound Hall of Fame stands as a lasting tribute to the great personalities—human and hound alike—that have enriched the sport. Housed inside the Hall of Fame are countless treasures, including memoirs, artifacts, pictorial displays, and, of course, plaques dedicated to the Hall of Fame inductees. For over thirty years, since the opening of the Greyhound Hall of Fame in 1973, retired racing Greyhounds have served as official greeters for visitors. Like their predecessors have done, Chig (Bets On Chig–BR) and Abby (RU Ms. Kim B–MU, WT, ST) greet dozens of people each day. Kathy Lounsbury, the administrative assistant, has been with the Hall of Fame since February 2001.

▲ During the racing-stock auction, Kansas-bred Greys Kanza Star was purchased for $20,000. By the end of the week, the eighteen-month-old pup was nearly a thousand miles away at Wheeling Island, one of the premier racetracks in the country.

▶ "If you don't buy him, you'll have to beat him!" shouts the auctioneer as he takes the final few bids for seventeen-month-old Craigie Demander. Purchased for $51,000, the pup went on to race at Wheeling Island. At the close of the auction, 174 Greyhounds had been sold for a total of $1,173,250, an average of $6,743 per pup.

With keen ears listening for cars driving into the parking lot, Chig waits on her oversized dog bed in the lobby for the next group of visitors to arrive.

FEEDING

GROOMING

A popular attraction, the Race America section of the Hall of Fame features dozens of illuminated panels, each one showcasing a different racetrack in the United States.

One rare historical artifact looks more like a small mining locomotive than what it actually is: an early lure cart designed by Owen Patrick Smith, the father of Greyhound racing. The cart was used at the Biscayne Kennel Club in the 1920s and operated on narrow-gauge railroad tracks.

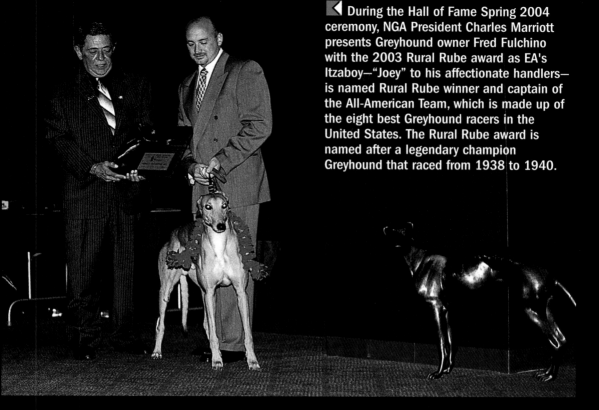

During the Hall of Fame Spring 2004 ceremony, NGA President Charles Marriott presents Greyhound owner Fred Fulchino with the 2003 Rural Rube award as EA's Itzaboy—"Joey" to his affectionate handlers—is named Rural Rube winner and captain of the All-American Team, which is made up of the eight best Greyhound racers in the United States. The Rural Rube award is named after a legendary champion Greyhound that raced from 1938 to 1940.

Another Rural Rube and All-American winner, thirteen-year-old Dougy (EJ's Douglas–BI, MU, SL) served as an official greeter for the Hall of Fame until his passing in July 2004. Of all the Greyhounds who have served as greeters, Dougy was the first to have been previously inducted. Visitors often noticed how the old boy carried himself—he knew he was a champion. Given the track star's old age, Dougy spent much of each day on his favorite bed in the office, leaving most of the greeting duties to Chig and Abby. Outside in the turnout pen, it was a different story—he would run the legs off his younger female companions.

The yellow Abilene Greyhound Park sign next to Old Highway 40 has become a local icon, welcoming breeders and visitors to the facility. The Abilene Greyhound Park, which opened in September 1975 and was known as the Kansas Greyhound Park until 1987, is a year-round schooling racetrack that offers puppy and lure training. The cozy-looking grandstand seats one hundred patrons—small by pari-mutuel racetrack standards—and is filled to capacity during the semi-annual puppy stake races.

107

▲ During the early stages of training, pups are hand-slipped on the backstretch, and they run the racetrack by themselves to further develop their focus on the lure and the route to the escape turn. By ingraining the routine, free of the distraction caused by traffic and bumping from other Greyhounds, pups develop a feel for the racetrack and for chasing in circles.

◀ With a pair of pups owned by local breeder Jeff Cole on the racetrack, Maurice Flynn Jr., owner of AGP, operates the lure using a rheostat throttle in the corner of the grandstand. Because no wagering takes place at the schooling racetrack, there are no odds or payoffs to display and therefore no tote board behind the backstretch.

▶ Next in their training, pups are introduced to the shortbox, a starting box located halfway up the front stretch. The starting position is moved back from the turn until, finally, the pups are ready to start from the 5/16th starting box. Pups schooled at pari-mutuel racetracks are hand-slipped from this same location midway down the front stretch.

Later in the morning, AGP schooling assistant Joe Copeland lends a helping hand at the escape turn.

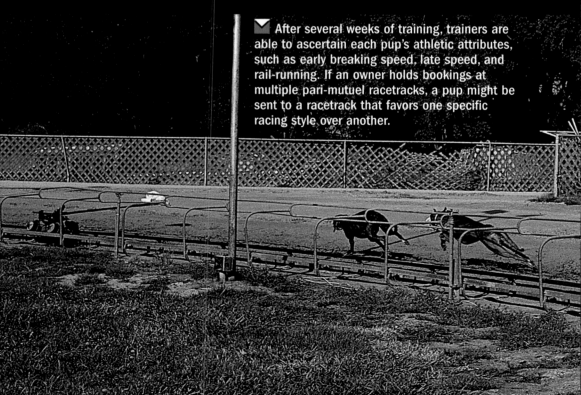

After several weeks of training, trainers are able to ascertain each pup's athletic attributes, such as early breaking speed, late speed, and rail-running. If an owner holds bookings at multiple pari-mutuel racetracks, a pup might be sent to a racetrack that favors one specific racing style over another.

▲ Holding pens located at the first turn temporarily hold the pups during the short time after their races, before they are loaded back into specially made trailers. Immediately after being walked off the racetrack, the pups are sprayed with water for a cool-off, and special attention is given to washing sand out of the pups' feet and eyes. A trainer loads the pups into a trailer for a quick ride home. Trailers such as this one are used for short hauls. If, however, the Greyhounds were being moved over a long distance, such as from one racetrack to another, a trailer with climate control would be employed.

In the years since the Texas Greyhound Association's schooling racetrack opened, a great deal of research and experimentation has gone into improving safety for the racers. Changes in banking elevation on the curves, depth of cushion, types of sand, and amount of water in the sand, as well as experimentation with using launch pads in front of the starting boxes, have led to positive results.

CHAPTER 6

LONE STAR RISING

6

In 1933, the Texas Legislature passed a bill legalizing pari-mutuel wagering, which ironically came about as a result of two Thoroughbred racetrack patrons being arrested in 1931 for openly gambling on the horses. The publicity from the court case gave racing advocates a voice in the media and also in the state capital. Prior to the pari-mutuel bill, Thoroughbred and Greyhound racing in the Lone Star State was a hit-and-miss affair, with local sheriffs raiding facilities, closing racetracks, and arresting patrons whenever the officers felt the need (or desire) to do so.

The Galveston Kennel and Fair Association operated the first Greyhound racetrack five years before pari-mutuel betting became legal, hosting its first

Dream and reality: Overcoming numerous obstacles to be granted a state license, the Gulf Greyhound Park finally opened its doors on November 11, 1992—two years after the Valley and Corpus Christi Greyhound Parks unleashed their racers in November 1990.

and only meet in 1928. Although the association did not return in 1929, two other groups soon established themselves in El Paso and Houston, both opening in 1932. Of the two, only the Missouri City Kennel Club in Houston managed to hold on until the pari-mutuel bill was passed into law. By 1935, Greyhound racetracks in Dallas, Houston, and San Antonio were in operation. In the following year, the Arlington Kennel Club opened in the Dallas/Fort Worth area.

Unfortunately for the racetracks, backing for the pari-mutuel bill began to evaporate in the state capital, forcing racing supporters to scramble to maintain their still-new legal status. Despite their best efforts, racetracks began closing down in reaction to failed lobbying efforts; by the time the bill was finally repealed in 1937, only one racetrack—in Dallas, operated by the Sportsman's Greyhound Racing Association—was still in operation, but it promptly closed after the bill was repealed. Although the sport of Greyhound racing was rapidly expanding in other states, such was not the case in Texas and would not be the case for another fifty years.

During the November 3, 1987, general election, Texans approved the return of pari-mutuel wagering in Galveston, Cameron, and Nueces counties, all of which are located along the Gulf Coast. Of the three racetracks eventually built, the Valley Greyhound Park in Harlingen was the first to celebrate its inaugural race, which occurred on November 14, 1990. The facility cost $16.2 million to construct and covered nearly 80 acres.

On November 15, 1990, a day after the Valley Greyhound Park reintroduced the sport to Texans, the Corpus Christi Dog Track hosted its grand opening. Holy Tera, a red brindle male just under two years old, won the Corpus Christi inaugural race in front of thousands of patrons. The racetrack, which cost $20 million, was built to accommodate a thousand patrons in the grandstand and an additional seven hundred in the clubhouse. The kennel buildings were built strong and on high ground in case of a hurricane. The racetrack, essentially a canine storm shelter, also has a backup generator and stockpiles of dog food and fresh water. In the event of high flooding, all of the Greyhounds can be safeguarded inside the grandstand itself.

Sitting on 110 acres and costing over $55 million to build, the Gulf Greyhound Park in La Marque, located 235 highway miles north of Corpus Christi, opened its gates for the first time on a rainy November 10, 1992, as the third and final Greyhound racetrack in Texas. With a parking lot big enough to accommodate eight thousand vehicles, the racetrack has seen over 10 million patrons visit the facility as of 2009.

Like its two newer counterparts, the Valley Greyhound Park originally enjoyed a large patron base, but despite that fact, it lost millions of dollars and was forced to close on September 30, 1995, $5 million in debt. For the next four and a half years, the racetrack sat idle while the Corpus Christi and Gulf Greyhound Parks soldiered on. In 2000, the Sam Houston Race Park purchased the Valley Greyhound Park, renaming it Valley Race Park. On March 17, 2000, Greyhounds returned to the facility during a memorable reopening experienced by thousands of patrons.

While the sport of Greyhound racing in Texas has experienced setbacks in recent years—namely with the closing of the Corpus Christi Dog Track in 2007 and of the Valley Race Park in 2009—the Gulf Greyhound Park along with the Texas Greyhound Association (TGA) is forging ahead. On April 7, 2009, the Texas Racing Commission approved the sale of the closed Corpus Christi Dog Track to the LaMantia family, who also owns licenses to a pair of Texas-based Thoroughbred racetracks. The reopening could bring nearly seventy new jobs back to the racetrack.

The TGA, which was founded by National Greyhound Association members originally seeking to again legalize pari-mutuel wagering in Texas, represents breeders' interests in legislative action and promotes the sport of Greyhound racing within the state. The TGA facility, which schools seventy-five to one hundred pups from roughly two dozen local and regional breeding farms each weekday, is the only such schooling track operated by a racing association in the country.

Located in Bruceville, a small town situated about 18 miles south of Waco, the Texas Greyhound Association's facility includes a schooling track and five kennel buildings capable of housing over one hundred Greyhounds.

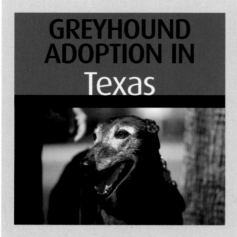

GREYHOUND ADOPTION IN Texas

A staunch supporter of Greyhound adoption, the Gulf Greyhound Park has found homes for over two thousand Greyhounds through its adoption program. During the annual Adoption Reunion Parade held each November, more than a thousand retired racers and their owners return to visit the racetrack. In 2006, more than fifteen hundred Greyhounds attended the parade—it was the biggest turnout to date.

An advocate for the dogs as well, the TGA hosts annual adoption summits, bringing together owners, breeders, and adoption volunteers to share new ideas and discuss concerns. During the second annual adoption summit on February 4, 2005, twenty representatives from Gulf Greyhound Park, Heart of Texas Greyhound Adoption, Greyhound Adoption League of Texas, Hill Country Greyhound Adoption, and Greyhound Pets of America's North Texas, Houston, and Central Texas chapters met at the TGA facility to discuss wide-sweeping issues concerning adoption efforts. One such idea considered the scenario of an adoption organization in need of an extremely active male, for example, while another organization had the right type of dog being fostered by a volunteer. The two organizations could then transfer the retired racer between each other, thus reducing wait time for the adopter and also freeing up space for another retired racer waiting at a breeding farm.

Diane Whiteley, executive director of the TGA, summed up the meeting by stating, "In a perfect world, three or four groups would be constantly ready to pick up Greyhounds from farmers, owners, or kennels." She continued, "Adoption is key to keeping the sport viable. We create allies for our business and create new fans. Helping adoption groups benefits the dogs, owners, breeders, racetracks, and the sport."

Other adoption organizations, including Greyhounds Unlimited, continue to find homes for retired racers in Texas.

▲ Barking, jumping, and howling for fun, energetic five-month-old pups (CTW Westward Ho–Bobarann) greet the morning—and their feeders—with unleashed fanfare at David and Janele Peck's breeding farm in Stephenville.

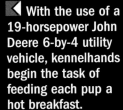

◀ With the use of a 19-horsepower John Deere 6-by-4 utility vehicle, kennelhands begin the task of feeding each pup a hot breakfast.

◀ David Peck, an advocate of Greyhound safety, strives to fine-tune the racing surface by adding specific amounts of water to the sand-and-clay composite at a specific time before racing starts. David's goal is to provide the Greyhounds with improved footing while racing on a consistent surface. A grading tractor enters the far turn on David's schooling racetrack, pulling a dragging apparatus made up of a cutting blade and automobile tires. By maintaining a specific compaction rate with water in the racetrack surface, slippery and boggy spots are eliminated.

117

▶ While racetrack employees verify ear-tattoo numbers in the foreground, an associate veterinarian examines one-year-old RGS Dawn to make sure she is free of ailments and ready to race. Hours later, the fawn-colored pup took second place in her fifth grade-M race.

◀ Built at a cost of $52 million, the four-story Gulf Greyhound Park was the third and final Greyhound racetrack opened in the Lone Star State and is an especially safe place for dogs to live. The kennel buildings are elevated by 20 feet and were constructed to withstand Category Four hurricanes.

▶ Under a colorless sky, leadouts prepare to load a field of grade-D racers into the starting box for a 550-yard race.

With a commanding lead, Bob's Comedy (number 6) rounds the first turn during a grade-D race. From maiden to retirement, this pup spent his entire racing career at Gulf Greyhound Park—eighty-eight races in all.

In a rare view seen from the infield, eight grade-B racers led by one-year-old Gil's Laredo pass by a pull-out curtain and charge around the first turn.

In a veterinary clinic located inside the paddock, veterinarian Charles Hoover checks out Pride Jasper for signs of injury. Because the clinic is located at the racetrack, Greyhounds are able to receive prompt medical care in the event of an accident.

▲ Three-year-old Huston Street wears both a number-1 racing jacket and an imposing look of confidence during a grade-B post parade. After 195 races—all in Texas—Huston Street retired in March 2007.

▲ Comparing ear-tattoo numbers against registration information, the Corpus Christi Dog Track racing secretary confirms the identity of Cl Soaring Free while his kennelmate Ezee Eddie Bob looks over the competition. Coincidentally, the two Texas-bred pups started their racing careers on the same day, February 3, 2004, at the Gulf Greyhound Park, and both ended their careers the same way, by refusing to leave the starting box during a race.

▶ Waiting their turn— and not so patiently— Greyhounds from multiple racing kennels stand outside the paddock as the ear-tattoo check and weigh-in get underway.

▲ BC's Homefree (number 1) lives up to his name as he streaks ahead of seven other grade-AA racers—the best the racetrack has to offer. At the height of his racing career, the 73-pound pup managed a third-place finish in a stake race just weeks later.

▲ After making a clean break from the starting box, a field of grade-AA racers accelerates onto the chute. With some wins earned by the length of a nose—or less—a clean break can make all the difference.

◀ Showing great promise, one-year-old TNJ Dingo (number 8) takes command of a grade-C race—his only one before moving on to grades B, A, and AA. A year and a half later, the golden pup was a genuine fan favorite at the racetrack.

125

◀ Not quite a year old, Jetta Becky is taking her first steps into the world of racing. By running the racetrack solo—without the bumping and competition of other dogs—the pup is able to acquaint herself with the racetrack environment free of distraction.

▲ Running on the outside of the racetrack, eleven-month-old TNJ Lemondrop (number 6) races past another Texas-bred Greyhound in her thirty-one-second pursuit of Breezy, the mechanical lure at the Corpus Christi Dog Track. With the leaders in sight on the first turn, the amber-clad pup makes her move.

▶ Like a bolt of lightning out of a Texas thunderstorm, TNJ Lemondrop streaks into the escape turn after winning her first grade-J race—a grade the 60-pound speedster left behind for good after this race. Her next race was against much faster dogs in grade C.

127

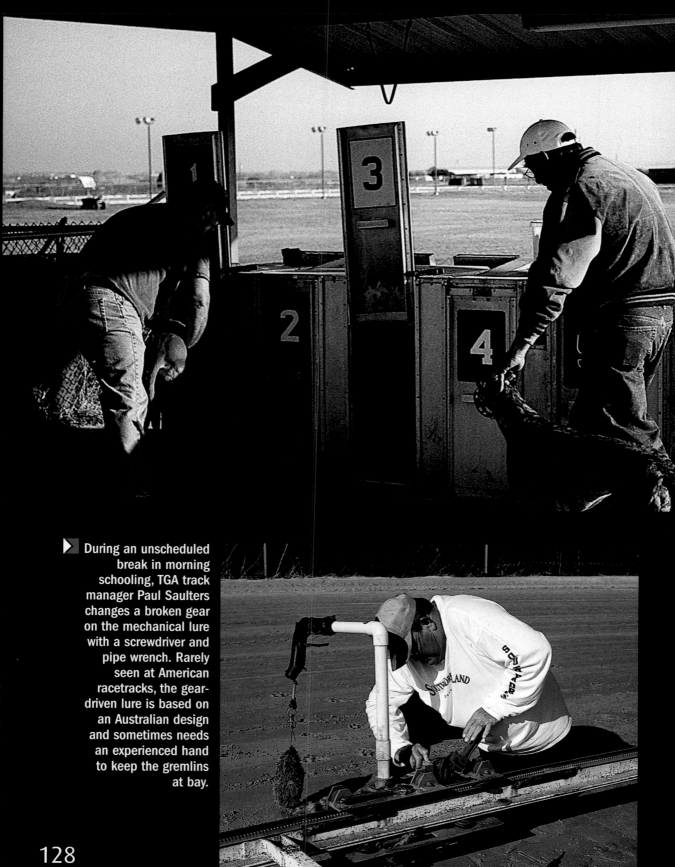

▶ During an unscheduled break in morning schooling, TGA track manager Paul Saulters changes a broken gear on the mechanical lure with a screwdriver and pipe wrench. Rarely seen at American racetracks, the gear-driven lure is based on an Australian design and sometimes needs an experienced hand to keep the gremlins at bay.

◀ Still learning the ropes and yet ready for the next phase in their schooling, a pair of pups is loaded into the starting box for a genuine race at the Texas Greyhound Association's schooling racetrack. The empty number-2 box serves as a buffer to give the pups some space while accelerating down the chute.

▶ Gathered for the first annual All-Breed Fun Run at the TGA facilities, people listen to ground rules that will keep their sighthounds as safe as possible while racing. The TGA co-sponsored the event with the Rapid Transit Greyhound Club to raise awareness of adoption efforts and to promote safe Greyhound racing.

When the starting box opens, three retired racing Greyhounds shed their couch-potato ways for one last shot at glory on the 550-yard racetrack. Adoptive owners standing along the backstretch cheered enthusiastically as their dogs sprinted past.

▲ An Afghan Hound is a surprising sight as he breaks from the starting box and sprints down the chute and onto the racetrack. While a break from the norm of what is usually seen on the racetrack, this aristocratic-looking dog is right at home, having previously raced at amateur racing and coursing events where starting boxes were utilized.

◀ Looking every bit like their larger cousins, a trio of Whippets races down the front stretch and toward the first turn. While the hobby of Whippet racing may appear similar to Greyhound racing, the two sports are inherently different. During Whippet racing events, owners strive to gain titles and ribbons without legalized pari-mutuel wagering.

Focused on the mechanical lure, three jacket-clad Afghan Hounds sprint around the far turn and onto the final stretch. While not trained on a Greyhound racetrack, the dogs are accustomed to lure coursing and chasing with the same enthusiasm as their quicker relatives.

▲ Tired yet immensely satisfied with herself, five-year-old retired racer Molly (Fire Next Time–MU, AP) takes a breather shortly after the TGA Fun Run. This successful event led to what is now the annual TGA Fun Run for Physically Fit Sighthounds and Retired Racing Greyhounds.

A hotshot on the high plains, Hallo Sky Oak (number 4) paves the way for a field of grade-M racers as they speed around Mile High Greyhound Park's first turn and onto the backstretch. After reaching grade AA at the nearby Cloverleaf Kennel Club roughly five months later, the pup finished out his career at the Post Time Greyhound Park in Colorado Springs, Colorado.

CHAPTER 7

ROCKY MOUNTAIN MOSAIC

Greyhound racing was still in its formative years when it first came to Colorado in 1927. Barely a footnote in the history of the sport, the Lakeside Park Kennel Club operated for just one meet at Denver's Lakeside Amusement Park. Twenty years later, as the 1940s were coming to a close, a road to legalization was being paved by racing enthusiasts and the Colorado Racing Association that led to the passing of a pari-mutuel bill on November 2, 1948.

With financial backing in place, construction began almost immediately on three racetracks: Lake Avenue Park (later renamed Pueblo Greyhound Park) in Pueblo; Mile High Kennel Club (later renamed Mile High Greyhound Park) in Commerce City, a suburb of Denver;

Symbolized with green clovers, the Cloverleaf Kennel Club was actually named after the nearby Highway 87 cloverleaf—present-day Interstate 25 and East Eisenhower Boulevard.

and Pike's Peak Park (later renamed Rocky Mountain Greyhound Park and then Post Time Greyhound Park) in Colorado Springs. All three racetrack operators planned to open their respective facilities by the summer of 1949.

The first night of official schooling races at the Mile High Kennel Club got underway on July 6, 1949, while construction workers hurried to complete the $750,000 facility. Under the threatening skies of that evening, officials, trainers, and two hundred and fifty curious patrons watched as the first of three hundred Greyhounds took to the new racetrack. Within weeks, the number of patrons watching the evening schooling races had climbed to more than five thousand each night.

Greyhound racing made its official Colorado debut at Pueblo Kennel Association's Lake Avenue Park on July 15 in front of an estimated crowd of three thousand racing fans—some of whom had traveled from Kansas, Arizona, and New Mexico to witness the event. Pancoast, a two-year-old pup who had previously raced at the Washington Park Racetrack in Phoenix, Arizona, won the tightly matched Pueblo Inaugural Handicap. At the conclusion of the ten-race card, patrons had wagered $18,589.

At the Mile High Kennel Club racetrack the following day, stubborn mechanical problems with the tote board forced George F. McCarthy, president of the kennel club, to delay the grand opening by nearly a week. Meanwhile, thousands of patrons continued to attend the free official schooling races.

The second Greyhound racetrack to open in the Centennial State did so on July 21 as twenty-five hundred patrons filled Pike's Peak Park for the Rocky Mountain Kennel Club's inaugural race. Ruth Etting, a well-known radio personality and actress of the time, presented a wreath of roses to City Clerk, the winner of the night's main event. Slightly better than Lake Avenue Park's handle, $23,046 was the total wagered that night in Colorado Springs.

After a false start and a great deal of local fanfare, the Mile High Kennel Club kicked off its inaugural season on the balmy evening of July 27. Racing officials expected fourteen thousand people to attend the premiere. By the start of the first race, 16,328 patrons had filled the racetrack, setting a national attendance record for a Greyhound racetrack's opening night. Shortly into the three-hour-and-forty-minute program, the troublesome tote board once again failed, causing a great deal of confusion for the patrons and likely reducing the night's handle by $5,000. In contrast to the confusion of opening night, subsequent nights ran much more smoothly.

In the spring of 1955, a fourth Greyhound racetrack set down roots on the high plains of eastern Colorado: the Cloverleaf Kennel Club. The racetrack, located north of Denver, near Loveland, derived its unusual name from the nearby Loveland-Greeley highway cloverleaf, a symbol of modernization during the early days of highway expansion.

Trimmed out in a fresh coat of Colorado Red Rock paint, the racetrack opened to the public on May 16 for the first day of official schooling races. Just three days later, however, racing officials were forced to put a brief halt to the schooling races after torrential rains dumped an inch of water onto the racetrack's surface, short-circuiting the electrical lure system.

Unlike the Mile High Kennel Club's inaugural race, when the heat of summer made patrons swelter, a bone-chilling wind from the north blew on the Cloverleaf Kennel Club during its grand opening on May 27. The pre-race ceremonies included a contest to name the mechanical lure; a local racing fan, Mrs. Hilma Bruce, was awarded a Greyhound pup for submitting the winning name, "Whizmo."

Colorado's fifth and final Greyhound racetrack, the Interstate Kennel Club, celebrated its inaugural race on February 13, 1971. The $2.5-million plant was 40 miles east of Denver, near the small town of Byers, and offered grandstand seating for six thousand. During the grand opening, 6,672 patrons stuffed themselves into the plant, forcing security officers to

After a racing stint at Denver's Mile High Greyhound Park, Dee Dee (MH Deannti) was returned to the breeding farm and produced a single litter of ten puppies. Her adoption was arranged by Greyhound Pets of America's Northwest chapter. At age eleven, the former speedster and brood matron lived in Salem, Oregon, 1,300 miles away from her old racetrack.

close off the parking lot and creating a mile-and-a-half traffic backup on Interstate 70. The racetrack operated for two thirty-day meets each year, one starting in February and another in November, until its ultimate closure in 1991. The Interstate Kennel Club meet was thereafter held at the Mile High Greyhound Park until its closure seventeen years later in 2008.

Unfortunately for racing fans in Colorado, the Cloverleaf Kennel Club ended racing with its 2006 season. It briefly remained open as an Off-Track Betting facility, or OTB for short, before the entire facility was sold for redevelopment. On June 28, 2008, the Mile High Greyhound Park ceased its operations, bringing a close to all Greyhound racing in the Centennial State. Only time will tell if the sport will make a comeback in Colorado.

Toolie (R's Snowbird–SC, CD) with fellow retired racers Snoopy (Black Marian–CD), Bessy (Inkan Bless Bess–CD), and Terri (Motor Rite Date–CD) on Christmas Day. When the pups came in from their afternoon turnout, they found stockings full of special treats waiting for them.

▼ Somewhat unusual in design when compared to other breeding farms, a row of covered shelters is used to protect the pups from the elements at the breeding farm owned and operated by Peggy and Daryl Brumage. The shelters, which are shaped similar to mountaineering tents designed to withstand extreme winds, hold up remarkably well in poor weather. During summer months, the strategically placed roof keeps the sunlight at bay.

◀ Located just down the road from the old Interstate Kennel Club racetrack near Byers, Colorado, is this breeding farm and family. The Brumages' farm is a state-of-the-art facility built up from humble beginnings dating back to the 1960s. These days, grown sons Ronnie and Johnny help out while manning their own breeding farm next door. In a long-since unused kennel building, Daryl recalls old times while holding a two-month-old puppy (Chick's Racey–Endless Trix). The kennel was originally built as a World War II-era barracks structure and was once owned by Greyhound Hall of Fame inductee Paul Sutherland.

🔼 As on any breeding farm, the daily routine follows a strict timetable that begins at dawn with the first turnout of the morning.

NO FOOD OR DRINK IN PADDOCK

◀ Eight Greyhounds from the Hadley/Johnson kennel pause at Cloverleaf Kennel Club's paddock doors. Just inside, a small numbered brass tag showing the race number and starting-box position is assigned to each Greyhound. The racers are also weighed while they make their way through the paddock. The weight of each Greyhound is published in the racing program along with weight history of his previous six races. If a Greyhound consistently loses a few pounds between weigh-ins, the symbol WL, for "Weight Loser," will appear in that dog's racing lines. Weight loss is important to Greyhound handicappers wagering on the races because it can affect how fast a racer will run.

◄ Greyhounds are loaded into the jinny pit, also known as a lock-out kennel, shortly before a matinee card. This particular kennel, which is unusual in design and unique to the Cloverleaf Kennel Club, spreads outward from the paddock in two directions with an outdoor walking area in the middle. In July 2004, during the off-season, the jinny pit was pressed into emergency service when the Larimer Humane Society Animal Protection and Control asked the racetrack to temporarily house thirty abandoned Labrador Retrievers who needed shelter.

▲ Shortly before their races, Greyhounds are walked outside the paddock to loosen their muscles. Looking somewhat like point-of-call markers on a racetrack, fire hydrants are strategically placed for inevitable potty breaks.

Having just graduated from the maiden grade, Boc's Lil Comet stands poised and ready for her first grade-C race. Throughout 2005 and 2006, the fawn-colored speedster slowly migrated to the south, racing at the Mile High and Phoenix Greyhound Parks and eventually ending up at the Caliente Racetrack located in Tijuana, Mexico.

A grade-TB race is moments away as leadouts walk their assigned Greyhounds out of the paddock. The T in TB represents a mixed-grade race, so in this race, grades B, C, and D are represented. Two-year-old Pat C Doughboy (number 2) finished the race in second place.

▲ Hugging the rail and holding onto the lead during an official schooling race, Pat C Charade holds off his racing competitors as he exits the final turn. Five days later, he raced in grade C after a nearly month-long hiatus. A true Coloradoan, the pup was whelped at a breeding farm near Longmont and ran in sixty-five races, all in the same state.

◀ Putting the "whiz" into Whizmo, veteran lure operator Pete Jeffries drives the mechanical lure using a rheostat throttle. If the lure speeds up too quickly and pulls away from the Greyhounds, they might give up the chase. Conversely, if the lure moves too slowly and the dogs catch up, one or more of the racers might end up injured.

During an official schooling race, pups from different kennels break from the starting box and race off the chute and onto the racetrack. In the distance, snowcapped foothills mark

Two powerful grade-A contenders, Keys Tanner (number 4) and CB Expression (number 7) sprint down the front stretch near the wire. After Cloverleaf Kennel Club's 2005 season finale, both dogs continued to race at the Mile High and Post Time Greyhound Parks during the same time. However, they never again competed against one another.

In a dazzling display of purebred athleticism, a field of grade-A racers explodes onto the first turn. Well behind the leaders, Pat C Buttondown (number 5) was trailing in last place. Thrusting himself past the other dogs on the backstretch, the blue-brindle hotshot did not yield, earning a win by two lengths. By October 2007, when Pat C Buttondown finally retired from racing, he had seen an amazing 201 races.

Year-and-a-half-old Kay V Say How is ten days away from his maiden race. For the moment, official schooling races will do. The racetrack at the Cloverleaf Kennel Club favors early speed in Greyhounds and was a good match for the pup, who was explosive on the front stretch. Two years later, the black Greyhound was racing at the Mardi Gras Racetrack in Fort Lauderdale, Florida.

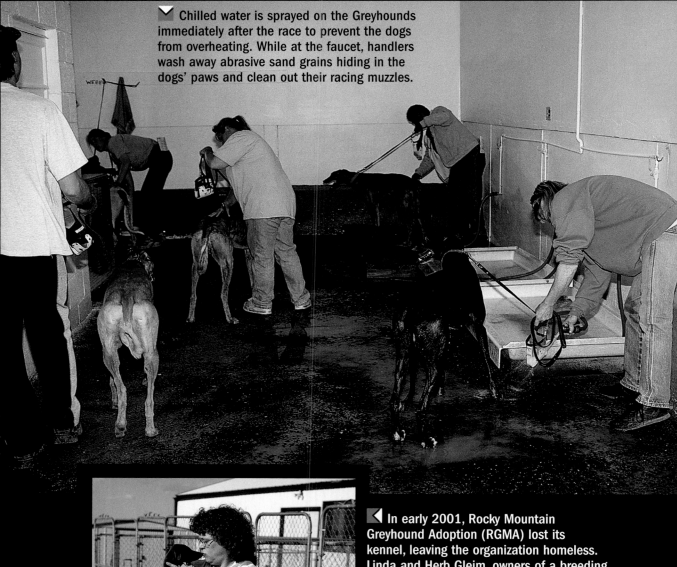

Chilled water is sprayed on the Greyhounds immediately after the race to prevent the dogs from overheating. While at the faucet, handlers wash away abrasive sand grains hiding in the dogs' paws and clean out their racing muzzles.

In early 2001, Rocky Mountain Greyhound Adoption (RGMA) lost its kennel, leaving the organization homeless. Linda and Herb Gleim, owners of a breeding farm located near Brighton, Colorado, came to the proverbial rescue. Along with numerous local businesses, they donated goods, money, and labor to give the troubled group a new home. As a result, a brand-new adoption kennel was built on the Gleims' breeding farm and opened in January 2002 at a cost of $35,480. Here, RMGA vice president Jan Woll enjoys the company of Cowboy (Fortified Power–Macs Aunt AJ), a rare blue-colored two-month-old puppy. Tragically, the puppy was whelped with a serious physical abnormality that claimed his young life just months later.

148

The adoption kennel not only houses retired racers and boarders but also is utilized three or four times a year to raise litters of puppies. Goofing it up, a two-month-old pup (Fortified Power–Macs Aunt AJ) plays with a kennelmate during an outdoor romp. The white-and-blue pup was named Soldier Pet but was never individually registered to race. Instead, Soldier was adopted as a pet through RMGA.

Half of the eighteen runs inside the adoption kennel are occupied by Greyhounds waiting for adoption while the remainder are being used to board retired racers—as well as other breeds at times—to help make ends meet. On average, the adoption organization finds homes for roughly 150 to 175 Colorado-bred retired racers each year.

149

Three-year-old Sabrina's Wish stands on Multnomah Greyhound Park's front stretch as her racing competitors have their stretchvests and muzzles checked by the patrol judge. At the time of this photograph, the red-jacketed pup had over a year's worth of experience, starting at the Pueblo Greyhound Park in Pueblo, Colorado. She continued to race in every grade for another year before being adopted by a loving family.

CHAPTER 8

NORTHWEST TRADITION

Simply put, the Multnomah Greyhound Park represented the epitome of Greyhound racing in the Pacific Northwest. Originally the Multnomah Kennel Club (MKC), the racetrack was known as a Portland, Oregon, icon for more than seventy years and was a great supporter of Greyhound adoption until the day it closed in 2004. The Oregon Greyhound Association, a nonprofit organization made up of Greyhound breeders within the Beaver State, continues adoption efforts by working closely with local adoption groups to help find homes for all retired racers whelped in Oregon.

Painted in traditional Pacific Northwest colors and clad with silhouettes of racing Greyhounds, Multnomah Greyhound Park's grandstand has become a Portland, Oregon landmark. Opened in July 1957, the racetrack was an immediate success despite the fact that it was located about ten miles outside Portland.

The Multnomah Kennel Club was established in 1933 shortly after a bill was passed in the Oregon Legislature to legalize pari-mutuel wagering. During the same year, the MKC reached an agreement with the Multnomah Athletic Club to operate Greyhound racing at its then-vacant Multnomah Civic Stadium located in downtown Portland. Conversion of the stadium happened quickly, allowing nightly Greyhound racing to begin on May 25.

Ten races were scheduled for the first night, with the Governor's Inaugural Trophy Contest highlighting the evening activities. Despite a large crowd in attendance, the low amount of money wagered was disappointing. The amount from the second night was even less. Luckily for the kennel club, the dismal first few weeks of racing did not prove to be a sign of things to come, for the making of Greyhound-racing history was just around the corner.

On August 11, 1933, eleven weeks after MKC's grand opening, more than thirty-five thousand patrons attended the inaugural running of the Multnomah Kennel Club Derby. It was estimated by the kennel club that another seven thousand to eight thousand people were turned away at the gates. The attendance record set that night has yet to be broken by a Greyhound racetrack anywhere in the world.

Twenty-two years after that tumultuous first year of operation, the MKC found itself without a racetrack when the Multnomah Athletic Club decided to convert its stadium to house professional baseball games and did not renew its contract with the kennel club. While the Greyhounds were running their final races at the Multnomah Civic Stadium in 1955, a 91-acre site near the town of Fairview was selected as the new location for the racetrack. To raise the $1.4 million needed for the land purchase and construction costs, the kennel club offered 886,000 shares of public stock.

Much to the shock of the kennel club, the contractor building the new racetrack fell into bankruptcy, and construction came to an unceremonious halt with months of work left unfinished. Scrambling madly to find a temporary home for the upcoming 1956 season, MKC found an unlikely home at the Portland Meadows Thoroughbred racetrack, 12 miles north of the old stadium site. To facilitate Greyhound racing at Portland Meadows, officials had a smaller racetrack constructed within the larger infield of the Thoroughbred course.

MKC quickly found a new building contractor, and work resumed on the Fairview racetrack, with construction progressing steadily toward the July 1957 completion date. As the final brushstrokes of paint were being put to the grandstand, qualifying races started for the nearly nine hundred and fifty Greyhounds that were being housed in a new kennel compound located immediately east of the grandstand. On July 15, 1957, the racetrack officially opened and was named Fairview Park. The new facility, located 12 miles to the east of the Multnomah Civic Stadium and about 10 miles outside the Portland metro area, was an immediate success despite Portland residents grumbling that the racetrack had been built too far away from the downtown area.

More recent ownership of Fairview Park, now known as the Multnomah Greyhound Park, has managed to change hands not once, but twice. On March 12, 1998, R.D. Hubbard Enterprises, Inc., sold the facility to Arthur McFadden, an Oregon real estate investor and longtime racing enthusiast. Three and a half years later, on October 26, 2001, Magna Entertainment Corporation (MEC)—a Canada-based owner and operator of several Thoroughbred racetracks—finalized an agreement with McFadden to purchase the operations and to lease the real estate on which the track was built.

On December 23, 2004, MEC announced it would not renew its lease of the Multnomah Greyhound Park and that no further races would be conducted there. After operating the

At the Schaffer Farm, located outside Portland, this precious eight-week-old puppy (Forbes Sasquatch–Alley Gator) was eventually given the name BD Golden Girl. After beginning her racing career at the Naples–Fort Myers Greyhound Track in Bonita Springs, Florida, she returned home for a time to compete at the Multnomah Greyhound Park before finishing her career back at the Naples–Fort Myers racetrack.

Multnomah Greyhound Park for just four seasons, MEC closed the book on one of the oldest and most storied racetracks in the history of Greyhound racing. At the end of 2008, MEC found itself with assets of near $1.5 billion and liabilities of approximately $959 billion. On March 5, 2009, the company filed for bankruptcy in the United States Bankruptcy Court for the District of Delaware.

GREYHOUND ADOPTION IN Oregon

Despite the closing of the racetrack, breeding and adoption continue on as if nothing happened. Because of lingering efforts to find a new facility to race Greyhounds, local breeding farms have continued to operate, sending their pups to racetracks as far away as Florida. The dogs ultimately return to Oregon after retirement and are placed in an adoption kennel maintained by the Oregon Greyhound Association (OGA). Located at the since-closed Multnomah Greyhound Park, the lively kennel offers a small reminder of the racetrack's glory days.

Two adoption organizations, Homes for Hounds and Greyhound Pets of America's Emerald Pacific chapter, place Greyhounds from the adoption kennel with families throughout the Pacific Northwest. Working independently of the OGA, two Greyhound Pets of America chapters, Northwest and Coastal Oregon, take in retired racers from outside the region, creating a good balance. In May 2006, ten Greyhounds came from as far away as Juarez, Mexico, and were placed into the Northwest chapter's adoption program.

Surrounded by pine trees that stand over 100 feet tall, the 24-acre Schaffer Farm is located near Estacada, Oregon, and is one of the most scenic breeding farms in the country. Kirk Schaffer and his wife, Lisa, started the farm in early 1980 with a single pen to house their first two Greyhounds, littermates Fully Involved and Firefighter. During morning kennel duties, Kirk takes some precious time out to play with a litter of eight-week-old puppies (Forbes Sasquatch–Alley Gator).

A pair of five-month-old pups (Wigwam Hoss–PHX Utep) casually enjoys breakfast. Sharing one feed pan between four or five pups helps the young dogs develop socialization skills that they will use their entire lives—including lives as pets.

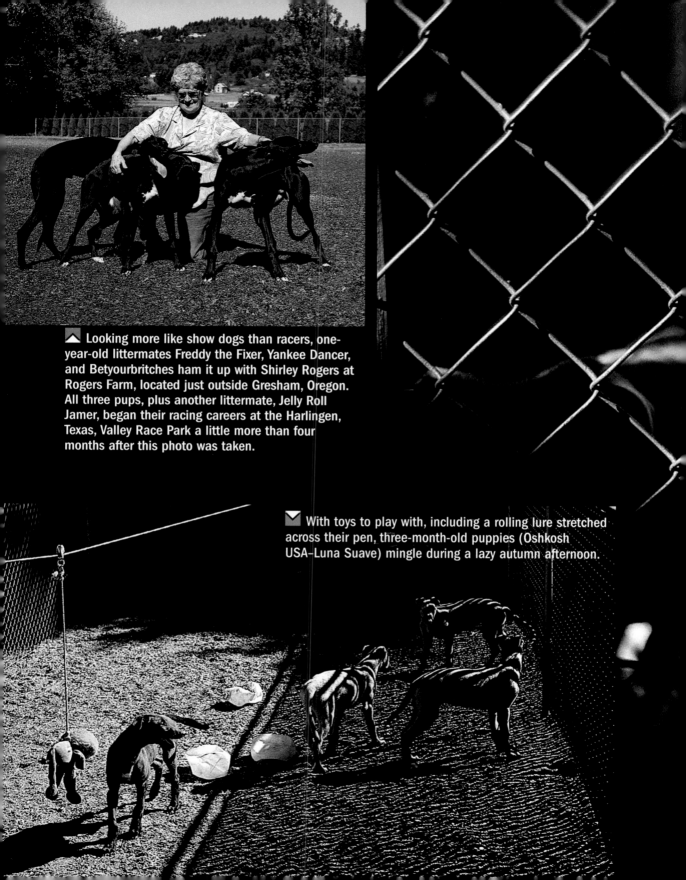

▲ Looking more like show dogs than racers, one-year-old littermates Freddy the Fixer, Yankee Dancer, and Betyourbritches ham it up with Shirley Rogers at Rogers Farm, located just outside Gresham, Oregon. All three pups, plus another littermate, Jelly Roll Jamer, began their racing careers at the Harlingen, Texas, Valley Race Park a little more than four months after this photo was taken.

▼ With toys to play with, including a rolling lure stretched across their pen, three-month-old puppies (Oshkosh USA–Luna Suave) mingle during a lazy autumn afternoon.

▲ Perking up at the sounds of yipping dogs from the other side of the breeding farm, one of the puppies casts an intrigued glance through a fence to investigate. This puppy was named Scat Man Do and eventually raced seventy-four times in Oregon, Texas, and northern Mexico.

157

The Multnomah Greyhound Park was the last of over forty Greyhound racetracks throughout the country to employ a bugler to play "Call to Post" before each race. Other racetracks simply broadcast a recording.

Forever synonymous with Multnomah Greyhound Park will be the name Murray Kemp. For half a century, he served as the president and general manager who guided the kennel club through its storied history. A plaque honoring his many achievements stands next to the main entrance.

◄ Leadouts walk Express Star (number 4) and Zodiak Zeke (number 5) onto the racetrack as the post parade gets underway moments before a grade-M race. Within months, Express Star was racing at the Apache Greyhound Park in Arizona while Zodiak Zeke was at Florida's Hollywood Greyhound Park. The following summer, both dogs returned to Oregon to continue their racing careers at the Multnomah Greyhound Park.

The patrol judge inspects the racing jacket on Bob's Shawna moments before a matinee race. If a race jacket is not put on correctly, a Greyhound can hook one of his hind legs inside the coat, causing an accident. Because of this, the patrol judge carefully checks to make absolutely sure that every jacket is secure and properly worn by each Greyhound.

Kid's Jaguar gets a kindhearted pat from his leadout as they wait for the six remaining Greyhounds to get their blankets inspected moments before a grade-D race. On their days off, most leadouts from Multnomah Greyhound Park drive out to the area farms to play with the Greyhounds they have come to know and adore.

In their third race against each other, Ryan Expressway (number 1) and Pikes Chuckylove (number 7, left, number not visible) appear to be almost egging each other on as they are walked to the starting box.

◀ Oregon-bred Dougie Fresh (number 8) leads seven other Oregon-bred racers moments before earning a grade-D win for the Washburn Kennel. At the conclusion of the 2003 meet, Dougie Fresh was sent to the Apache Greyhound Park in Apache Junction, Arizona.

◀ Leadouts stationed behind the first turn watch closely for anything that can go wrong, ready to spring into action, as Doubt The Dawn leads a field of grade-C racers down the front stretch. Built with safety in mind, the top 8 inches of the racetrack consists of Columbia River sand and blow sand from the Oregon Coast. If a dog falls, a cushion of layered sand with specific water content most often prevents an injury.

▼ Elegant even at full throttle, TX's Sue appears to fly down the home stretch as she races the wind during a grade-E race. The two-year-old pup got her start in racing at the Valley Race Park in Harlingen, Texas, moving north to the Multnomah Greyhound Park in April 2003.

▲ JNB Mojet Lady (number 5) drives hard but just cannot break out from the middle of the pack. The number-five position is one of the worst to draw for this very reason. With racers on her right and left, JNB Mojet Lady is jammed up with no running room.

▶ In an amazing display of canine locomotion, Oregon-bred Sitbackangrin (number 3) just holds off another Oregon-bred Greyhound, Where's My Keys (number 7), to capture a close grade-M win.

▲ On the home stretch, the left side of the field starts to break apart and JNB Mojet Lady finds some running room next to the rail. Alas, she runs out of racetrack, and the win goes to Marilyns Missle (number 6, not visible), who easily takes the victory by three and a half lengths.

▲ Oregon Racing Commission veterinarian Dyrk Scholingman carefully watches each Greyhound as the field is walked to the cool-off area just moments after another matinee race. Dr. Scholingman keeps a close watch for any sign of possible injury. From his vantage point on the first turn, the veterinarian is able to watch each race with the fewest blind spots on the racetrack. If there is an accident during a race, he will be able to give medical care within minutes. The high level of care that Greyhounds receive while racing is nothing new to those who work in and around the racing kennels; however, it is rarely seen or appreciated by outsiders. At Multnomah Greyhound Park, the welfare of each and every Greyhound was paramount.

After each performance and out of the public's eye, a post-race urine sample is collected from the winner—along with others selected at random—to check for any illegal drugs or stimulants in the Greyhound's system.

In conjunction with Greyhound Pets of America's Northwest chapter, the racetrack hosted a special event known as "Make a Fast Friend Day" to help find homes for retired racers. During the meet-and-greet, GPA volunteers introduce several recently retired Greyhounds to dozens of potential adopters. With the combined efforts of racetrack employees and adoption volunteers, several retired racers found new homes as a direct result of the event.

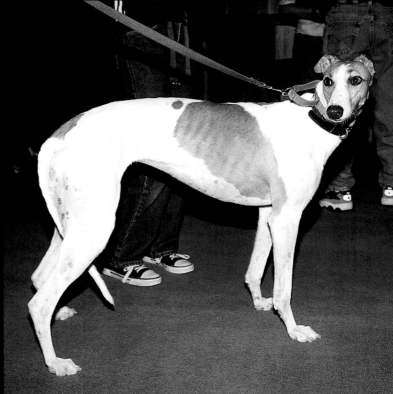

▲ During the meet-and-greet, Creamy (Whats Up Baby–HO, PU, MU) wastes no time in introducing herself to everyone present. The four-year-old retired racer did not have to wait long; she was adopted shortly after the event.

◀ In a celebration of companionship and homecoming, hundreds of Portland-area residents, along with their retired Greyhounds, converge at the racetrack for an annual retired racers' reunion. The event starts with a parade of retired racers on the racetrack, followed by a luncheon on the third floor of the grandstand, with proceeds going to local adoption groups. Almost lost in a sea of smiling faces are employees of the racetrack and trainers who revel in seeing so many old friends at once. Some Greyhounds literally jump for joy when reunited with their former trainers.

▲ In a gesture of appreciation, Multnomah Greyhound Park general manager Jeff Grady and animal welfare coordinator Patti Lehnert welcome each person walking in the parade. Likewise, Patti's retired racer Cassie (Windy Cass–EB, HO, MU) welcomes her former competitors in turn—although from a relaxed position. After the parade, reunion participants are encouraged to stay and enjoy the afternoon races. Once inside the grandstand, a man holding onto a pair of retired racers turns to a friend and says, "Wow! We are in Greyhound heaven."

▶ Nearly two hundred people, along with their retired track stars, head around the first turn and onto the front stretch as each Greyhound is announced by racing and pet name. The parade began shortly before the Sunday matinee card, and as a result, some of the racetrack's regular patrons filtered outside to watch the procession up-close. The lighthearted joking and wisecracks coming from the patrons prompt rounds of laughter from everyone within earshot.

Wendy Heidt, a volunteer from Greyhound Pets of America's Northwest chapter, and ten-year-old Dee Dee (MH Deannti-MH) relax on a merry-go-round. While recounting their many years together, Wendy jokingly asks how Dee Dee could have gone from the whirly-gig to a merry-go-round in such a short time.

CHAPTER 9

EXTRAORDINARY PETS

The words *Greyhound adoption* conjure up visions of retired racers playing in backyards and then sleeping away the rest of the day, adoption kennels manned by tireless volunteers, meet-and-greets at pet-supply stores on Saturday afternoons, and gigantic Greyhound gatherings that last for days. Yet, there is so much more.

The history of Greyhound adoption actually goes back to the very beginning of the sport—although on a much smaller scale and with an exceptionally smaller number of Greyhounds whelped each year. Throughout the twentieth century, owners

JR (HR's Holding On–MU), owned by George Mildeberger, enjoys another pleasant summer afternoon, just like countless afternoons before. After a nice walk around their Beaverton, Oregon, neighborhood, they found a cool, shady spot in their backyard to relax and enjoy retirement, just as it should be.

and trainers would sometimes give favorite Greyhounds who were no longer competitive to friends or relatives to whom they thought they could trust the dogs' care. Unfortunately, without guidance in how to care for Greyhounds' special needs, such informal adoptions often ended in tragedy because the new owners simply did not know how to keep a retired racing Greyhound safe from hazards.

The idea of formally adopting out retired racing Greyhounds to the general populace began to take root during the 1970s as the sport dramatically expanded. Prior to that time, the attitude of the general public toward racing Greyhounds was less than favorable. People preferred to own herding or hunting dogs—"respectable dogs." Breeds such as the Collie and German Shepherd had been popularized with the likes of Lassie and Rin Tin Tin. Greyhounds, however, were largely thought of as killing machines that could not bond with people and would destroy personal property.

As the Greyhound adoption movement slowly gained momentum during the 1980s and especially the 1990s, generalized misconceptions about the breed began to fall away as adoption volunteers properly educated the public about the Greyhound's disposition—often one person or one family at a time. Many potential adopters found themselves amazed by the gentle and loving nature of these dogs.

On April 4, 1987, the practice of Greyhound adoption entered a new phase with the formation of the nationwide Greyhound Pets of America (GPA) organization. During its first year of existence, GPA grew to twelve chapters located across the country and found homes for roughly one hundred Greyhounds. Later that same year, on October 18, GPA had its first official meeting in Abilene, Kansas, with representatives from just four chapters in attendance. By 1993, the ever-growing organization was adopting out more than three thousand retired racers annually.

In 2002, GPA launched a program that strives to realize seven thousand adoptions per year, thus establishing the goal of a 100-percent nationwide adoption rate for retired racers. A year later, the collective GPA chapters and subchapters were finding homes for more than a dozen former racers every day. Because of GPA's efforts, combined with those of independent adoption organizations, 90 to 93 percent of all racing Greyhounds are either adopted as pets or returned to their respective breeding farms to become sires and dams.

During the past decade, adoption efforts within the sport have also gained momentum. The American Greyhound Council, a joint effort of the National Greyhound Association and the American Greyhound Track Operators Association, was founded to ensure the welfare of Greyhounds. It currently grants over $120,000 of its annual budget to adoption organizations.

On a local level, racetracks themselves donate significant funds to help retired racers find homes. Many racetracks even have adoption kennels within their secure, on-site kennel compounds. Jim Gartland, the former general manager of the Woodlands Racetrack in Kansas City, Kansas, estimated that his racetrack donated around $70,000 each year to cover operating costs of the on-site adoption kennel.

In 2004, pedigree buff Dennis McKeon came up with the idea of donating purse winnings from individual racing Greyhounds to help raise funds for adoption organizations. Known as RaceForAdoption, the consortium became a reality when Greyhound owner and breeder Larry Birnbaum agreed to donate the future winnings of Whistler's Stud—a pup of extremely high potential. Communicating via online discussion boards, Greyhound lovers purchased shares, which led to $20,000 being raised before Whistler's Stud ran his first race. The program morphed into a real moneymaker for adoption organizations; eleven racers owned by Everytime Enterprises, Monte Hoopes, David and Rebecca Johnson, Henry Howe, and Angela Wilson-Taylor took to the racetrack for the first RaceForAdoption effort. By 2009, the consortium had raised more than $150,000 for eight different adoption organizations around the country.

While Greyhound adoption efforts have made great strides during the past twenty years, certain problems continue to plague volunteers. For many adoption organizations, the biggest hurdle to overcome is the basic transportation of retired racers from faraway racetracks. Because many adoption organizations are located in states that do not host Greyhound racing, the transportation of retired racers to adoption kennels can be a multi-state and expensive endeavor—especially when transporting retired racers from Florida to western states.

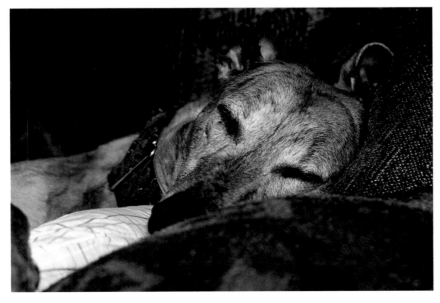

The king of his couch, Homer (Four Day Weekend–MU) power-naps during a lull between his backyard romp and dinnertime. An Oregon native, the seven-year-old brindle boy has lived in Salem since retirement.

To ease the burden of delivering Greyhounds to locations far removed from southeastern racetracks—such as California and the Pacific Northwest—Halfway Home Greyhound Adoption transports retired racers from their home base in Tulsa, Oklahoma. Largely funded by donations from breeders, online auctions, and RaceForAdoption, the organization delivered more than 1,750 Greyhounds to numerous locations between 2002 and 2006.

With some twenty thousand retired Greyhounds adopted as pets every year in the United States, events known as "Greyhound gatherings" have exploded in popularity and range from small-scale gatherings in city parks to retired racers' reunions at racetracks to gigantic multilayered events. The biggest of such gatherings, Greyhounds Reach the Beach, takes place every Columbus Day weekend in Dewey Beach, Delaware. The gathering first took place in 1995 and was attended by fewer than a hundred people and sixty-five retired racers. In recent years, thousands of visitors have flocked to the resort destination with roughly three thousand Greyhounds, marking the breed as one of the most popular pets in America.

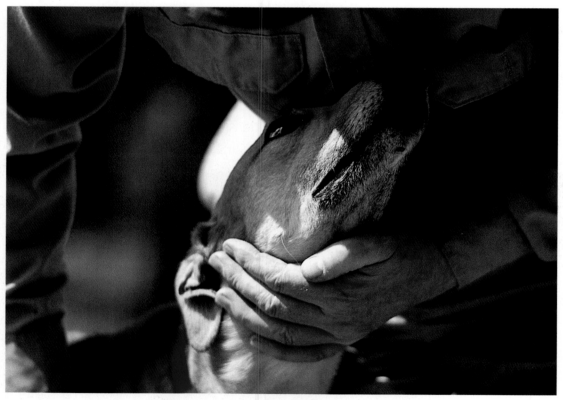

Retired racers transition easily into being pets because of the tender care that they receive while racing. An old saying that originated within the sport of Greyhound racing best describes the sentiment: "Doing right by the dogs." It is a universal truth shared by breeders, trainers, racetrack employees, adoption volunteers, and adopters alike.

▲ Under a vast and threatening sky, volunteers of Greyhound Pets of America's Rocky Mountain chapter, along with dozens of regional adopters, meet in Missoula, Montana, for an annual Greyhound gathering. Roughly an hour later, the covered picnic area resembled an oversized sardine can, crammed with people and Greyhounds as torrential rains passed over the area.

◀ Ignoring the loud rain blasting against the pressed-metal roof, seven-year-old Chester (RRS Winchester–CL, PU) claims a dog bed as the ever-adapting Montanans start a lively fundraising auction.

With ears raised, ten-year-old Belle (Cebo Light Belle–CD) listens to the distant sounds of children playing in a Spokane, Washington, city park. After a racing stint at the nearby Coeur d'Alene Greyhound Park, Belle was adopted by a Spokane resident and never left the area.

GPA volunteers (LEFT TO RIGHT) Judy Pfaff and Cindy House and president Sheri Glaspey meet at an old train station in Missoula for a walk with their retired racers as the Greyhound gathering winds down. Given Montana's large size—it's the fourth biggest state in the nation—get-togethers such as this are special treats for members of the group because they do not happen often.

At the rustic looking Greyhound Pets, Inc., adoption kennel located in Post Falls, Idaho, nineteen retired racers just arrived from Denver, Colorado. Once off the rig, the muzzled dogs were led to the turnout pen directly behind the kennel. Curious about their new surroundings, the Greyhounds checked out the volunteers and then proceeded to sniff everything in sight, interrupted only by numerous potty breaks, where the dogs were followed by several volunteers with pooper-scoopers at the ready.

▲ One by one, each dog is sprayed for possible fleas and ticks and given preventative medication for worming and a booster for kennel cough. While this is going on, a volunteer records the Greyhounds' information, including their new collar numbers, for an electronic database. Like any well-run adoption kennel, Greyhound Pets, Inc., will not change the dogs' daily routine. Breakfast, turnout, and dinner times stay the same, as if they were still in racing kennels, thus minimizing stress that they might endure.

▶ Leader (Majestic Leader–WD, MU, VG, AP, TU) has just arrived at the adoption kennel with twenty-three other speedsters from Tucson, Arizona. Representing a significant milestone for Greyhound Pets, Inc., the shy pup became the four-thousandth retired racer adopted out by the organization. By 2007, four years after Leader was adopted, the volunteers had found homes for another seven hundred Greyhounds.

1

▲ Perched high above the Palouse farmlands of eastern Washington, Janice Mosher and her retired racers, Walter (Street Waltz–RM, PU, MU, MH) and Roslyn (Rapido Roslyn–TU), gaze from the summit of 3,612-foot-high Steptoe Butte. From the vantage point, Janice and her friends can see for nearly 200 miles in every direction.

▲ Just outside Cheney, Washington, near the northernmost fringe of Palouse country, Garrett Voorhees and his daughter, Jennifer, walk their three Greyhounds—Amy (Ambitious Amy–AP, TU), Icy (Atomic Ice Queen–PH, TU), and Ceppy (Mr. Ceppy–FL, MH, CL, PU)—down a forgotten and dusty farm road. The rolling wheat fields seem to go on forever with nary a house, telephone pole, or any other hint of modern civilization in sight.

Clearing four Greyhounds in a single bound, Chey (Cheyanne Bowman–MB) performs the world-record Greyhound jump as she leaps over her Dancing Greyhound teammates—Safire (Indio Kwik Kick–PB), K.C. (Moon Mt Casey–OP, OR, PE), Mist (Alexandria Mist–JC, MB), and Beauty (NC Beauty–FL, NF, SM)—at the Coeur d'Alene Greyhound Park in Post Falls, Idaho. This team of acrobatic Greyhounds performs at racetracks and adoption events across the country.

Safire effortlessly glides several feet off the ground as she performs the hand-jump act between Gil and Kathleen Gilley, the drill team's two human performers. This stunt actually came about from an entirely unrelated act. During a performance at the Phoenix Greyhound Park, Safire was asked to perform a hand jump but insisted on jumping between Gil and Kathleen, so they joined hands and allowed Safire to do it her way.

185

▲ Like a Broadway star, Mist gives a big bow to her adoring fans. During performances, the bow act is used both to warm up the girls before their stunts and to indicate to the crowd that a stunt

▲ Looking like a shiny black skyrocket, Beauty jumps over a foam noodle held above Kathleen's head.

◀ Beginning in the late 1980s, U-Haul launched a program to celebrate the uniqueness of each state by placing large graphics on the sides of their moving vans and trucks. For Kansas, the Greyhound Hall of Fame was highlighted with a striking image of racing Greyhounds, and the graphic quickly became a rolling icon for Greyhound lovers across the country. One such moving van is randomly found in Cheney, Washington, as Nancy Slaughter and her four retired racers—Cracker (Brazo Cracker-PU), Rose (Prima Smokinrose-MU, PU), Whisper (Whisper Snow-PU), and Brake (Daybreak Snow-PU)—enjoy a fleeting moment of sunshine during an otherwise dreary day.

▲ Lucy (Aurelia Ran–MU, CD) is full of Halloween spirit, as the night of ghosts and goblins approaches in Cheney, Washington. So much for the proverbial black cat scaring people—this Greyhound has that job all to herself.

Dino (Bella Alano–TU) and Abby (Courtney Rush–PH, AP, TU) gaze out the window as another winter storm slams into the little town of Cheney, Washington. Moments later, they grew tired of the view and laid down for the night. With baseboard heaters blasting away in the little apartment, they slept warm and sound until morning.

Diane Branch and her two special boys, three-year-old Dale (San Diego Dale–AP) and one-year-ld Ty (WD's Ellsworth–TU), are all ears as they clown around in Spokane, Washington's Manito Park.

As the sun sets on a long day, Homes for Hounds president Rayetta Holder prepares to load recently retired Alice (EMC Orderupalice–PU, PH, AP, MU) into her dog truck after a meet-and-greet n Kennewick, Washington. The start of a three hour drive back to Multnomah Greyhound Park's

According to official stud books, only one in every fifteen hundred to two thousand Greyhounds will sport a dark red coat. Cocoa (Thatsmisterwoman–SL) is one such dog. In order for a dark red puppy to be born, each parent must carry the gene for the rare color and at least one parent must be black, blue, or dark red. While on a walk in Steel Lake Park in Federal Way, Washington, Cocoa takes a breather.

At the same park, Sara Spears and dogs Slim (Slo Slim–CD) and Shooter (Burger Shooter–CD) walk the shoreline of Steel Lake. Seven years have passed since the senior-age Greyhounds raced at the Coeur d'Alene Greyhound Park. Their retirements have been long and richly lived.

▲ In a rare moment of stillness, Mocha (Bit The Bullet–PU) contemplates pouncing on another stuffed toy in her Auburn, Washington, home. Not afraid of keeping high-strung Greyhounds in check, Sheila Parr adopted the brindle pup shortly after she was returned by a less-experienced adopter. Sheila jokingly wonders if Mocha's name should be changed back to her kennel nickname—Twitchy!

▲ Chris Brown and dogs Jacob (Hard Knox Taker–MU), Jasmine (Frozen Coat–PU, MU), and Desi (Ico Desi–MU) take in an explosion of springtime colors as they walk among the cherry trees in front of the Oregon State Capitol Building.

Dr. Linda Lou Blythe, Associate Dean of the College of Veterinary Medicine at Oregon State University and co-author of the extraordinary and widely referenced book *Care of the Racing and Retired Greyhound*, admires her three-year-old retired racer, Scooby Doo (Baby Kelso–MU), in front of Magruder Hall, home of the college.

△ Five-year-old River (Eagle River–MU) presents a striking silhouette against the greenery of his Salem, Oregon, backyard.

▽ Barry Bottger and his two retired racers, Rush (Willowrun Rush–DP, GL, SS, DQ, BR) and Steel (Steel Eyes–MU), look over a restored B-17 bomber at the Corvallis, Oregon, airport. During the closing months of World War II, the Office of War Mobilization and Reconversion banned both Greyhound and Thoroughbred racing to save labor and critical materials for the war effort. The ban lasted five months and was lifted just one day after the German surrender on May 8, 1945—VE Day.

We're not in Kansas anymore! Having raced in Alabama, Arkansas, and Iowa, three-year-old Bailey (Greys Manateebay–VL, SL, BR) soaks in the sights and sounds of the Pacific Ocean near Newport, Oregon. The well-traveled pup was whelped at the Greymeadow breeding farm near Abilene, Kansas, and after a short racing career was sent to Greyhound Pets, Inc., for adoption.

Young and old, everybody loves a parade. Making a big showing, Greyhound Pets of America's Northwest chapter helps celebrate the Harvest Days Festival in Battle Ground, Washington, with a pet-shop inspired parade float. As the volunteers make their way down the main street, people cheer and wave while others shout, "Good work!"

Happy-go-lucky and available for adoption, Joey (Safe Man–MU) was fostered by a Greyhound Pets of America volunteer while waiting for a new family in Salem, Oregon.

▲ Pat Toman and her beloved thirteen-year-old Gal (Nevada Gal–HO, MU) take a moment to reflect on their wonderful years together. After a successful racing career in Florida and Oregon, Gal was kept by her owner to produce a few litters. Two years later, she was sent to the adoption kennel for retirement. After fostering her for a time, Pat finally adopted Gal in December 1999.

▶ Her racing years far behind her, six-year-old Becca (Becbob Pines–AP, MU) enjoys the retired life in her Portland, Oregon, cottage. With a fenced yard, another Greyhound to play with, and a human who caters to the dogs' every need, life is good.

DINO&ABBY'S ROAD TRIP

We've come a long way. Despite a shaky start in July 2001 with a used eleven-year-old Toyota Corolla, a manual-focus Canon A-1 camera, half a dozen miscellaneous lenses, and two energetic retired racers, an incredible journey into the world of Greyhound racing would become into a legacy of compassion and friendship.

Prior to their retirements, those racers—Dino (Bella Alano) and Abby (Courtney Rush)—were racing at the Tucson Greyhound Park in Tucson, Arizona. Unable to break his maiden,

Seizing a window of opportunity, we make a quick rest stop at Hyak, Washington, near the summit of Snoqualmie Pass. The rugged Cascade Mountains had just been hammered by a severe storm, closing Interstate 90 for two days. Less than an hour later, the pass was once again closed for avalanche control.

In high spirits during a sunny Christmas Eve in 2001 in Lincoln City, Oregon, Abby and Dino gaze upon the Pacific Ocean for the first time in their young lives. Earlier in the year, both dogs were thousands of miles away in the desert, racing at the Tucson Greyhound Park.

Dino retired at an early age. Dino's registered owner, David Blair, recalls, "Alano was awkward on the racetrack. He threw the turns by running wide and lifted his head while racing, very puppylike. If Alano could have matured, he might have been a real nice dog."

Abby, by contrast, enjoyed a racing career lasting just over two years. She ran in a couple of schooling races at the Phoenix Greyhound Park in December 1998, moving on to race in grade M at the Apache Greyhound Park in Apache Junction, Arizona. She ultimately

ended up at the Tucson Greyhound Park. Abby and Dino's retirement from racing, however, is where this story begins.

After moving cross-country from Tucson, in southern Arizona, to northern Idaho, the pups arrived at the Greyhound Pets, Incorporated, adoption kennel in April 2001, where Dino, in no uncertain terms, decided he was coming home with me. Abby joined our little family a few weeks later. In the short time leading to up the start of this book project, Dino and Abby lived normal lives like any other retired racer, but that would soon change.

After months of planning, my first photo shoot finally took place in a **Spokane, Washington,** backyard. It was a heavily overcast November afternoon and not one picture turned out. Obviously, there was a great deal to learn about photographing Greyhounds with a manual-focus camera, even when the dogs were standing still.

At first, our trips were limited to thousand-mile sojourns within the Pacific Northwest to photograph retired racing Greyhounds in places such as **Spokane, Portland, and**

Reliving old times, Dino and Abby take to the racetrack once again at the Abilene Greyhound Park. Two and a half years had passed since either had raced, but no matter—they are back home again and loving it. Moments afterward, AGP owner Maurice Flynn Jr. commented, "That white dog went right to the rail! Those dogs are retired?"

Seattle. While I enjoyed a great deal of success during those first months, one such trip to Portland, Oregon, nearly ended in disaster when debris on Interstate 84 punctured a tire on the old Corolla. With frayed nerves, we limped into The Dalles, Oregon, for a new tire.

I spent the warm summer of 2002 in **western Oregon,** photographing breeding farms, more retired racers, and matinee races at the Multnomah Greyhound Park. By September, it was time to branch out. With the help of several new friends, plans for a grand road trip to **Colorado** and then throughout the Midwest began to take shape. Over a ten-day span, we would visit the Mile High Greyhound Park in **Denver,** a breeding farm in eastern Colorado, the Abilene Greyhound Park, the Greyhound Hall of Fame, the Woodlands Racetrack in **Kansas City,** and finally Bluffs Run Casino and three breeding farms in **western Iowa.**

For someone from eastern Washington, a place with virtually no humidity, traveling across Kansas and Iowa in early September proved a genuine shock. The worst part of the trip came

when we tried to sleep in the car at a rest stop near the Missouri/Iowa border. At 3:00 a.m., it was still 90 degrees outside! That mistake would not be repeated, although it would not be the last time we would sleep in the car to save time and money.

Unfortunately for Dino and Abby, they would have to sit out the next two trips: a week-long journey to the **Florida panhandle** to visit St. Petersburg's Derby Lane, the oldest Greyhound racetrack in the world, followed by a trip to **Rhode Island** and **Connecticut** made possible by a travel expense grant from the Rhode Island Greyhound Owners Association.

Just two days after returning from Rhode Island in September 2003, I once again loaded up the old Corolla and we headed to the Midwest for a repeat road trip of the previous year. During our first trip in 2002, we had traveled 4,500 miles in ten days. This trip, however, would total more than 5,500 miles in ten days, including stops at half a dozen racetracks and as many breeding farms, and a two-day layover in **Abilene.**

Later, in April 2004, we returned to Abilene to photograph the NGA spring meet. During the final races of the meet, Dino discovered an ingenious way to break loose from the car, causing havoc while running back and forth along the backstretch. Luckily for me, the white terror did not interfere with the races taking place just yards away from him.

With the exception of one final road trip—a weekend visit to the Cloverleaf Kennel Club in April 2005—Dino and Abby's lives would finally settle back into a routine normal for most retired racers. Gone were the numerous visits to parts unknown and rough nights trying to sleep in the car. For a while, it appeared as though we had come full circle. Sadly, that was not to be. A terrible tragedy struck our little family in November when Abby suffered a seizure that took her young life. My companion was gone and I was heartbroken.

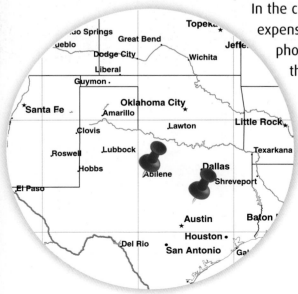

In the closing days of 2005, I was awarded another travel expense grant from the **Texas** Greyhound Association to photograph the TGA grounds, a breeding farm, and the three racetracks in the Lone Star State. Shortly after I returned to the Northwest, a new pup would join our family. Named Bailey, after her racing name, she would not know the wandering lifestyle that once felt normal for Dino and Abby—at least not now.

Country roads are taking us home after a trip into the agriculture-rich Palouse region of eastern Washington and northern Idaho. Even though the nearest Greyhound racetrack is over 300 miles away, the area is still known as Greyhound country. The college town of Pullman is home to the Pullman Greyhounds, a local high school situated in the heart of the Palouse.

Dino steals a few minutes of sleep before our departure on another 1,000-mile trip for the book project. By the time the day was over, we had traveled nearly 1,100 miles in sixteen hours and met forty other retired racers in Washington and Oregon.

Abby and Dino once again enjoy the sights and sounds of the spectacular Pacific Ocean near the town of Newport, Oregon, after a botched photo shoot with a no-show Greyhound adoption volunteer.

Electricity was in the air in Deer Lodge, Montana. While on our way to Abilene, Kansas, the skies lit up with a barrage of lightning that seemed to be drawn to the old electric-powered locomotive. A long, dark drive through central Montana and almost all of Wyoming was waiting for us.

Under a brilliant blue sky in eastern Wyoming, Abby and Dino stand among prehistoric-looking granite rock formations at the Vedauwoo Recreation Area in the Bow National Forest.

In a Council Bluffs, Iowa, hotel room that overlooks the Bluffs Run Casino and Racetrack, two road-weary Greyhounds take a breather during their 4,500-mile-long adventure through the Midwest.

Silhouetted against a wall of camellia in a Salem, Oregon, backyard, Abby soaks up the early morning sunshine shortly before heading north to the Schaffer breeding farm and the Multnomah Greyhound Park. Finally time to leave, Abby seems to ask, "Just another five minutes, please?"

The canine travelers play with new friends at Calabro Farm near Underwood, Iowa.

Racing at the old Black Hills Kennel Club in Rapid City, South Dakota, may be a thing of the past, but the spirit of the chase is alive and well. While exploring the grounds, Abby and Dino pause in front of the tote board, which, incredibly, remained after a decade of abandonment. In November 2002, a fire destroyed the grandstand, leaving few reminders of a once-busy place.

Off in the weeds, a set of vertical-open starting boxes offers a silent tribute to the breeders, trainers, spectators, and Greyhounds who gave life to the racetrack. Upon close inspection, the words SODRAC PARK are seen on the lip above the doors.

After traveling 4,500 highway miles in just ten days, Dino and Abby are glad to once again sleep in their own bed. Between December 2001 and April 2004, they traveled over 20,000 miles in total. In the end, there is no place like home.

Glossary

Adoption form: A signed contract between an adoption organization and an adopter of a retired racing Greyhound.

Adoption kennel: A kennel operated by an adoption organization, either independently or with the support of a Greyhound racetrack or breeding farm, to house retired racing Greyhounds waiting for future adoption.

Adoption organization: A nonprofit group of predominately unpaid volunteers who find homes for retired racing Greyhounds. There are currently over two hundred Greyhound adoption organizations in the United States.

Adoption volunteer: A volunteer who maintains adoption kennels, screens potential adopters, inspects homes of potential adopters, provides transportation, organizes fundraising events, maintains records, and places retired racing Greyhounds with adopters.

All-American Team: The eight best racing Greyhounds in the United States, selected annually by members of the American Greyhound Track Owners Association.

American Greyhound Council: A nonprofit organization supported by the National Greyhound Association and American Greyhound Track Owners Association that ensures the health, welfare, and safety of racing Greyhounds in the United States.

American Greyhound Track Owners Association: A nonprofit corporation made up of owners and operators of Greyhound tracks throughout the United States.

Announcer: A person who informs patrons at a Greyhound racetrack of post time, announces the name of each Greyhound during the post parade, calls the dogs' positions during the race, and announces the order of finish via a public address system.

Apron: The area between the grandstand and the outside edge of a racetrack. A fence separates the apron from the edge of the racetrack, and patrons may watch Greyhounds racing up close from this location.

Assistant trainer: A person designated by a kennel owner or trainer to assist the trainer in various kennel duties.

Backstretch: The straight section of the racetrack between the first turn and final turn, opposite the front stretch, that passes directly in front of the tote board.

Bertillon card: An identification card for each Greyhound that lists fifty-six unique physical identifying marks. The Bertillon card guarantees that a Greyhound listed in a racing program is the same dog in the race.

Bertillon number: A five-digit registration number assigned by the National Greyhound Association. The number is tattooed in each Greyhound's left ear and is recorded on the Bertillon card assigned to each dog. One Bertillon number is shared by an entire litter.

Blanket: An official racing jacket for a Greyhound, bearing a number from one through eight and a color that corresponds to the post position. In recent years, stretchvests have replaced blankets at some Greyhound racetracks.

Blinker muzzle: A racing muzzle that prevents lateral vision during a race. A blinker muzzle helps prevent an aggressive Greyhound from interfering with other racers; it must be approved by the state judge.

Bloodline: See Pedigree.

Blue slip: A registration certificate for individuals who have adopted a retired racing Greyhound; it includes the official National Greyhound Association registered racing name, pet name if desired, color, sex, two-generation pedigree, and Bertillon markings. A blue slip can be purchased only from the National Greyhound Association.

Box: See **Starting box**.

Box seats: Stadium-style seating in the grandstand.

Boarding kennel: A place where Greyhounds are sheltered, fed, watered, and/or trained in return for compensation.

Booking: A contract between a Greyhound racetrack and a racing kennel in which the racing kennel must supply a certain number of Greyhounds (state-bred if required), ready and available to race in various distances, for a racing secretary to draw on. In return, the racetrack provides kennel facilities and payment based on a points system for the top four Greyhounds in each race. A booking can be seasonal or permanent, depending on the racetrack's rules.

Brakeman: A racetrack official who prepares the lure for movement prior to a race and subsequently stops the lure at the end of a race. During a race, the brakeman is situated on the infield next to the first turn.

Breeder: A person who breeds Greyhounds for the purpose of pari-mutuel racing.

Breeders' association: An organized alliance of Greyhound breeders within the same state that promotes the welfare of Greyhound racing in its state.

Breeding farm: See **Greyhound farm**.

Brood bitch: A female Greyhound, no longer racing, who has been returned to a farm to be bred.

Bumped: A chart writer's term for a Greyhound who lost pace as a result of physical contact with another Greyhound while racing, usually in the first turn.

Calls: The position of each Greyhound at specific locations around the racetrack during a race.

Card: The set of races during one day, either matinee or evening, that is listed in a program.

Career record: A series of five numbers indicating a Greyhound's total number of starts, wins, places, shows, and fourth-place finishes—in that order—and a two-letter abbreviation indicating at which racetrack the starts were recorded.

Cart: The motor to which the lure is attached. Also called the lure motor. The cart travels on the infield side of the rail with an attachable arm that suspends the lure over the racetrack surface.

Celebrating Greyhounds magazine: A quarterly magazine for Greyhound owners and adopters, published by The Greyhound Project.

Chart: An official detailed record of each race showing finish, calls, odds, and abbreviated comments on each Greyhound's performance.

Chart writer: A racetrack official who compiles records of each race and writes abbreviated comments describing each Greyhound's performance during the races.

Checked: A term to describe a Greyhound who takes his attention off the lure during a race, sometimes causing the dog to slow down. Flash bulbs at night often cause Greyhounds to check.

Chute: The short section of a racetrack that extends from the starting box to the oval.

Circuit: Two or more Greyhound racetracks within a geographical area with complementary racing dates. For example, if one racetrack conducts racing between January 2 and June 30, a nearby racetrack would then operate between July 1 and December 30, allowing the same Greyhounds to race at both tracks.

Clerk of scales: The racetrack official responsible for weighing each Greyhound on a state-certified scale prior to racing. The clerk of scales keeps a list of all Greyhounds who have lost weight since the last time weighed and reports information, including any violation of state rules, to state judges.

Closed booking: A booking contract between a Greyhound racetrack and a racing kennel in which the kennel must be located within the racetrack's kennel compound or at a nearby location.

Closer: A Greyhound who starts a race out of competition for the lead and then speeds up on the final stretch to win, place, or show.

Clubhouse: An area within a grandstand or in a separate building next to the grandstand that usually offers table seating with personal closed-circuit monitors, a cocktail lounge, restaurant, and/or buffet. Access to a clubhouse may require a reservation and/or entrance fee, and patrons are expected to adhere to an appropriate dress code.

Cool-off area: Usually near the paddock, an area that allows trainers to safely cool down the Greyhounds immediately after a race by spraying cool water on their sides, as well as on their feet to remove sand.

Course: The distance of a race. Common distances include 5/16th-, 3/8th-, and 7/16th-mile courses.

Crate: A structure used to house individual Greyhounds in racing kennels, adoption kennels, and private homes.

Crow's nest: See **Judges' stand**.

Dam: The mother of a Greyhound.

Dead heat: An exact tie between two Greyhounds in the same race.

Derby: A championship stakes race.

Dog haul: Transporting of racing or retired racing Greyhounds from one racetrack to another or from a racetrack to an adoption kennel.

Doubleheader: Two cards or sets of races in one day.

Dragging: Smoothing and leveling the racetrack surface after a race to prevent injuries. This is done by a tractor pulling a resurfacing apparatus.

Dragging tractor: The tractor that pulls a resurfacing apparatus between races.

Draw: A random process that determines each Greyhound's starting position prior to a race.

Escape turn: The section of a racetrack where the lure disappears after a race is over; it is also the same location as the first turn at the beginning of a race.

Exacta: See **Perfecta**.

False start: When a starting box does not automatically open and the manual backup release fails on the first attempt.

Far turn: The point at which the racetrack turns left immediately after the backstretch. The far turn passes by the starting box immediately before transitioning into the home stretch.

Fast track: The condition of the racetrack surface that allows Greyhounds to achieve their best speed.

Favorite: A Greyhound expected to win and upon whom the most money is wagered.

Field: The number of entries in a race. Fields are comprised of eight Greyhounds per race unless one or more are scratched and not participating.

First turn: The point at which the racetrack turns left immediately after the front stretch.

Front stretch: The straight section of racetrack between the starting box and the first turn.

Futurity: A stakes race for two-year-old Greyhounds that usually involves an elimination series of prior races.

Grade: The system designed by Paul Hartwell that allows a Greyhound to race against other Greyhounds of similar speed and endurance. Grades range from AA (the fastest) to A, B, C, D, E, and Maiden. Greyhounds begin their racing careers in Maiden, advancing to higher grades each time they win a race. Similarly, Greyhounds who do not finish in at least fourth place, three times in a row, will be lowered a grade.

Grade AAT: A special grade designated for championship stakes races and hotbox events.

Grade T: A mixed-grade race. A letter always follows the T to indicate the highest grade allowed in the race; for example, grade TA indicates a mixed-grade race in which the highest grade is A.

Graded Maiden: A racing Greyhound in grade M, or Maiden, who has not won an official race but is allowed to move up to a higher grade at the trainer's request.

Grandstand: The main building at a Greyhound racetrack, consisting of bleacher-style seating, possibly a clubhouse, a restaurant, mutuel windows, the judges' stand, and offices.

Greyhound association: A nonprofit organization composed of Greyhound owners, kennel owners, trainers, and any other individuals who wish to promote Greyhound racing within their given state.

Greyhound farm: A privately owned and operated kennel in which Greyhounds are bred, whelped, raised, and trained for the purpose of pari-mutuel Greyhound racing.

Greyhound gathering: A gathering of people and their retired racing Greyhounds.

Greyhound Hall of Fame: Located in Abilene, Kansas, a hall of fame and museum celebrating individual accomplishments and the overall history of Greyhound racing in the United States.

Greyhound owner: A person or entity who owns a Greyhound and whose name is recognized by the NGA.

Greyhound Pets of America: A nonprofit corporation formed in 1987 whose sole purpose is to find homes for retired racing Greyhounds throughout the United States. GPA has forty-two chapters in thirty-one states.

Greyhound Review, The: A monthly magazine for the Greyhound racing industry published monthly by the National Greyhound Association.

Handicapper: A racing secretary or other official who analyzes racing cards and reports their findings to the public.

Handle: The total amount of money bet at a Greyhound racetrack each day; the handle is a barometer of how well the racetrack is doing financially.

Happy tail: A tail injured as a result of excessive wagging, sometimes resulting in amputation.

Helper: A person who assists a trainer and assistant trainer at a Greyhound farm or racetrack.

Hock: A joint halfway up a Greyhound's hind leg, akin to the human knee.

Home stretch: The straight section of racetrack between the final turn and the finish line.

Hotbox: A special championship stakes race that has the fastest Greyhounds racing against each other.

In the money: An expression referring to a Greyhound who finishes first, second, or third. A fourth-place finish will earn money for a racing kennel, but not for a wagering patron, unless the wager was a superfecta.

Inaugural: A first-season or a first-championship stakes race.

Infield: The grass-covered area situated inside the oval racetrack.

Interference: Intentional and physical contact from a Greyhound that hinders and/or obstructs another Greyhound during a race. Greyhounds that have been called for interference must run a schooling race before competing again.

Invitational: A championship-stakes race consisting of Greyhounds that have been invited to compete.

Jinny pit: See **Lock-out kennel**.

Judges' stand: The structure in which judges watch the racing; most are situated on top of the grandstand.

Juvenile: A special grade known as grade J, designated for pups moving up from a maiden win, that allows young Greyhounds to compete with other young Greyhounds of the same experience level. Greyhounds that have raced in higher grades cannot descend into grade J.

Kennel: A business that houses, feeds, and cares for Greyhounds under a contract with one or more racetracks.

Kennel collar: A plastic-coated collar designed to protect the fragile skin of a Greyhound.

Kennel compound: Multiple racing kennels in a protected area, often situated next to a racetrack.

Kennel owner: A person or entity that owns a racing kennel.

Kennel master: The person who, under the supervision of the paddock judge, unlocks the lock-out kennel immediately before weigh-in, verifies that the crates in the lock-out kennel are in good repair and free of any foreign materials, and oversees the leadouts removing the Greyhounds immediately before the post parade.

Kennel muzzle: A plastic device that is fitted over a Greyhound's mouth and is designed to help prevent a Greyhound from biting another. Kennel muzzles are used at Greyhound farms, racing kennels, adoption kennels, private homes, and adoption organization-sponsored gatherings in which retired racing Greyhounds freely mingle.

Kennel standing: A list published in a racing program that shows the number of starts and first-, second-, third-, and fourth-place finishes for each racing kennel.

Leadout: A handler employed by a Greyhound racetrack who parades the Greyhounds, places the dogs into the starting box, and retrieves Greyhounds who have been randomly assigned to him.

Length: A margin that is equal to the length of a Greyhound and used to indicate how far ahead or behind one Greyhound is to another during a race.

Lock-out kennel: Commonly referred to as the jinny pit, this is the kennel within the paddock that houses Greyhounds before races. This is the most sensitive area at a racetrack, and only specific personnel are allowed inside.

Lure: A stuffed toy in the shape of a bone or rabbit that Greyhounds give chase to during a race. The lure is attached to the cart, or lure motor, by an extendable arm.

Lure motor: See **Cart**.

Lure operator: An official who operates the lure during races. It is the lure operator's responsibility to keep the lure at a specific distance in front of the Greyhounds giving chase.

Maiden: A Greyhound who has yet to win an official race and is less than two years old.

Mainline: The primary hall or section of a grandstand, generally in front of the largest or only group of mutuel windows.

Marathon course: The longest racing distance. Most marathon courses are 7/16 th of a mile.

Matinee: Races conducted during daylight hours, often starting at noon or one o'clock p.m.

Meet: The span of time in a given year during which a Greyhound racetrack operates. For example, if a park conducted racing from January 1 to March 30 in 2009, that would be its 2009 meet. For a racetrack that operates year-round, January 1 to December 31 would be its meet.

Meet-and-greet: An event assembled by an adoption organization, sometimes at pet-supply stores, in which volunteers bring their retired racing Greyhounds to introduce to the general public as a way of promoting future adoptions.

Minutes to post: The number of minutes remaining before post time.

Morning line: A forecast of odds set by the racetrack handicapper that are published in the program and posted before wagering starts.

Mutuel clerk: A racetrack employee that sells wagering tickets to patrons.

Mutuel handle: The amount of money wagered during a card.

Mutuel window: The location in a racetrack where patrons can place bets.

National Greyhound Association (NGA): Established in 1906, the sole recognized registry for racing Greyhounds in the United States; it is made up of Greyhound owners, breeders, and trainers.

National Greyhound Night of Stars: A premier semi-annual racing event held at fifteen different Greyhound racetracks throughout the United States on the same night to help promote Greyhound adoption. Proceeds from wagering are donated to adoption organizations.

Nose: A win by the narrowest of margins.

Odds: A forecast of the order of finish in a particular race.

Off season: The time of year in which a Greyhound racetrack is not conducting races.

Owen Patrick ("O. P.") Smith: (1867–1927) The engineer who invented the mechanical lure system, patented in 1912 as the "Inanimate Hare Conveyor," and opened the first Greyhound racetrack in Emeryville, California, circa 1919. Considered the father of Greyhound racing.

OOP (out of picture): A chart writer's term used to describe a Greyhound who finished in or near last place and is out of the photograph taken as the lead Greyhound crossed the wire.

OTB (off-track betting): Legalized wagering outlets in which patrons can place bets on races at multiple racetracks throughout the country. OTB sites are the reason why a grandstand can be nearly empty, yet the racetrack still has a large daily handle.

Official results: Results of a race, authorized by the state judge.

Paddock: The area where Greyhounds are kept prior to racing.

Paddock judge: The racetrack official responsible for overseeing all activities in the paddock, including supervising the leadouts, identifying Greyhounds, and checking that muzzles and blankets are properly worn by Greyhounds prior to races.

Pari-mutuel: The system of wagering invented by Frenchman Pierre Oller in 1865 in which patrons wager against each other, not the house. All money bet, minus taxes and other takeouts, is divided among the winning participants. Pari-mutuel means "betting among ourselves."

Patrol judge: The racetrack official responsible for leading the post parade; conducting a jacket and muzzle inspection of each Greyhound in view of the judge's stand, starter, and patrons; and checking the starting box immediately after post time to make sure all Greyhounds have safely exited.

Pedigree: The lineage of a Greyhound.

Perfecta: A wager placed on two Greyhounds to win and show, in the correct order.

Photo finish: A near tie in which the image taken by the photo-finish camera must be used to determine the place of each Greyhound at the finish line.

Photo-finish camera: A camera that records the order of finish of each race and the racing times for each Greyhound.

Place: To finish a race in second place.

Plant: The entire Greyhound racetrack property, including the actual racetrack, grandstand, paddock, outbuildings, parking lot, and kennel compound.

Plant superintendent: An employee who oversees the maintenance of a Greyhound racetrack.

Points system: A method of payment to Greyhound owners and kennel owners for Greyhounds who finish in the top four of each race. The value of points is a barometer of the financial position of a Greyhound racetrack.

Point(s) of call: A Greyhound's position at specific locations on the racetrack that is later published in each Greyhound's chart. The point(s) of call vary with the distance of the race.

Post parade: A parade of the Greyhounds in a given race from the paddock onto the racetrack for patron viewing and an inspection of their blankets and racing muzzles by the patrol judge.

Post position: A Greyhound's starting-box position number, one through eight. A Greyhound's blanket or stretchvest number always corresponds with the post position.

Post time: The starting time of a race.

Post weight: A Greyhound's official weight as reported before a race and published in the program.

Program: A printed guide for a card, or a day's set of races, that includes detailed, compiled data that assists patrons in handicapping races.

Purse: The prize money distributed to the owners and kennel owners after a race.

Quit: A chart writer's term describing a Greyhound who stopped running during a race.

Quiniela: A wager placed on two Greyhounds to finish first and second, in either order, in the same race.

Racing commission: A state commission in charge of regulating all aspects of pari-mutuel racing within its given state.

Racing kennel: A kennel housing both active and inactive racing Greyhounds, usually located within a kennel compound.

Racing muzzle: A plastic device that is fitted over a Greyhound's mouth, designed to help prevent a Greyhound from biting or interfering with another during a race. A racing muzzle has a white tip to aid in photo finishes and protects the Greyhound's teeth as he attempts to bite the lure at the escape turn after the race.

Racing season: See **Meet**.

Racing secretary: A racetrack official who is responsible for reporting race conditions, assigning the weights for handicapping purposes, determining how many races of each grade are appropriate, receiving entries, and conducting random draws for post position, as well as the operation and organization of the race office.

Rail: A metal barrier, usually consisting of horizontal bars, that runs alongside the inside of the racetrack and on which the lure operates.

Rail runner: A Greyhound who prefers to run next to the rail.

Regrade: The act of adjusting a Greyhound's racing grade for reasons other than wins or losses, such as if a Greyhound is kept from racing for an extended time due to injury or is moved to a different racetrack with a higher or lower level of competition.

Refused: A chart writer's term describing a Greyhound who would not break from the starting box at the beginning of a race.

Retired racers' reunions: Events hosted by Greyhound racetracks in which people who have adopted retired racing Greyhounds are invited to return with their dogs.

Retired racing Greyhound: A Greyhound who is no longer racing and has been kept by his owner, farm owner, trainer, assistant trainer, or helper as a pet; kept at a farm to be bred; or adopted to a pet home through an adoption organization.

Rig: A trailer used to haul Greyhounds.

Rope track: A schooling racetrack in which the lure is connected to a rope that stretches around the inside rail. The rope is sandwiched by two automobile tires mounted on top of each other and is put into motion by the spinning of the tires, which is powered by an engine.

Ruled off: A Greyhound's status of being forbidden, by order of the judges, to continue racing in a particular state. Interfering or quitting twice usually causes the ruling.

Run(s): A long, narrow, fenced area, usually 15 feet by 100 feet, that is designed to allow Greyhounds to sprint in a straight path.

Rural Rube award: A coveted National Greyhound Association award given annually to the owner of the fastest Greyhound sprinter. The award is named after one of the fastest Greyhound racers of all time.

Scale room: A room located within the paddock where Greyhounds are weighed on a scale prior to racing.

Schooling race: A practice race without wagering. A schooling race can be unofficial, in which no results are kept, or official, in which results are kept and published.

Schooling racetrack: A racetrack that is used for training purposes. Most schooling racetracks are privately owned and located at Greyhound farms.

Scratch: To withdraw a Greyhound from a race prior to post time.

Show: To finish a race in third place.

Simulcast: A closed-circuit broadcast of real-time races from Greyhound racetracks. Wagering on simulcast races is the same as with live races.

Sire: The father of a Greyhound.

Slow track: The condition of the racetrack surface that does not allow Greyhounds to achieve their best speed.

Sprinter: A Greyhound who prefers to run short distances and achieves his best overall speed in a short distance.

Sprint course: The shortest racing distance, 5/16th of a mile or less.

Sprint path: See **Run**.

Squawker: A handheld device that makes a prolonged sound reminiscent of a small wounded animal. Squawkers are used to capture the attention of Greyhounds.

Stakes race: A championship race with a purse larger than those in ordinary races.

Starter: A racetrack official responsible for opening the starting box and overseeing the leadouts as they load the Greyhounds into the starting box, as dictated by the state judge.

Starting box: An electromechanical box with a gate that holds and positions the Greyhounds as a race begins to ensure that all Greyhounds start the race in unison.

State-bred: Refers to a Greyhound who was whelped in the same state in which he is racing and meets a specific set of rules dictated by an owners' association.

State judge: A state official who interprets and enforces the state rules, policies, and regulations of Greyhound racing.

Stretchvest: An elastic, tight-fitting racing blanket developed by Australian Nadine Wood.

Steward: A racetrack official that presides over a race meet and has jurisdiction over all other racing officials.

Straight bet: A wager for a particular Greyhound to win, place, or show.

Stud: A male Greyhound used for breeding.

Stud book: The yearly registry that lists breedings, individual litters, registrations, transfers, and other pertinent information.

Superfecta: A wager placed on the first four Greyhounds to finish a race, in order.

Tattoo number(s): Identification numbers placed inside both ears of a registered Greyhound. The right ear tattoo shows the date whelped and the order in which the dog was tattooed. The left ear tattoo is the dog's five-digit NGA registration number.

Ticket(s): A paper voucher for a wager showing the date, race number, Greyhound(s) wagered on, and type of wager.

Timer: An electronic timing device that is activated upon the opening of the starting box and is connected to the photo-finish camera.

Tote board: A large display board located directly behind the backstretch that displays the time to post, odds, pools, results, and payoffs for each race.

Track bias: A racetrack surface that favors a specific position or running style.

Track condition: The condition of the racetrack surface that impedes or assists the speed that Greyhounds can achieve. Water content, for example, of a racetrack has a major impact on the track condition.

Track record: The fastest recorded time in which a Greyhound completed a race on a given track.

Track superintendent: An official responsible for the proper upkeep of the racetrack.

Track veterinarian: A state-licensed veterinarian who oversees Greyhounds' health needs and administers immediate aid for all types of injuries.

Trainer: A person employed by a racing kennel who is responsible for keeping Greyhounds happy, healthy, and in top racing condition.

Training track: See **Schooling racetrack**.

Trifecta: A wager placed on three Greyhounds to win, place, and show in the correct order.

Triple dead heat: An exact tie between three Greyhounds in the same race.

Turnout: A time for Greyhounds at a Greyhound farm, racing kennel, or adoption kennel to relieve themselves, socialize, and play with other Greyhounds in a protected, fenced-in area called a turnout pen. Greyhounds are turned out four times a day.

Twin trifecta: A wager on the Greyhounds who will win, place, and show in the correct order in two designated races.

Unofficial results: Results immediately after a race that have not yet been authorized by the state judge.

Urine test: A post-race test of urine drawn from the winner—and others at random—to check for any illegal drugs or stimulants in a Greyhound's system.

Vetting: The spaying or neutering of a retired racing Greyhound by a veterinarian as preparation for adoption.

Wager: A bet, or the placing of a bet.

Weight allowance: The amount of weight permitted to be gained or lost from the official recorded weight of a Greyhound.

Weigh-in: The weighing of each Greyhound on a calibrated scale in the paddock; this is done by the clerk of scales prior to each race and is the last procedure completed before the Greyhounds enter the lock-out kennel.

Whelping: The birth of a Greyhound.

Win: To finish a race in first place.

Wire: The finish line of a race.

Whirly-gig: A device designed to teach a Greyhound to chase a lure in a circle.

Having raced 99 times in Arizona and Oregon, Cupid (Yukon Cupid–AP, MU) enjoys retirement in his Portland, Oregon, cottage. His old racetrack, the Multnomah Greyhound Park, is just a few miles away.

Greyhound Track Abbreviations

AP .... Apache Greyhound Park: Apache Junction, Arizona

AD .... Anthony Downs: Anthony, Kansas

BE .... Belmont Greyhound Track: Belmont, New Hampshire

BI .... Biscayne Greyhound Park: Miami Shores, Florida

BM .... Birmingham Course: Birmingham, Alabama

BH .... Black Hills Greyhound Park: Rapid City, South Dakota

BR .... Bluffs Run Casino: Council Bluffs, Iowa

CT .... Camptown Greyhound Park: Frontenac, Kansas

CC .... Corpus Christi Dog Track: Corpus Christi, Texas

CD .... Coeur d' Alene Greyhound Park: Post Falls, Idaho

CL .... Cloverleaf Greyhound Park: Loveland, Colorado

DB .... Daytona Beach Kennel Club: Daytona Beach, Florida

DP .... Dairyland Greyhound Park: Kenosha, Wisconsin

DQ .... Dubuque Greyhound Park: Dubuque, Iowa

EB .... Ebro Greyhound Park: Ebro, Florida

FL .... Flagler Greyhound Track: Miami, Florida

FV .... Fox Valley Greyhound Park: Fox Valley, Wisconsin

GG .... Gulf Greyhound Park: La Marque, Texas

GL .... Geneva Lakes Kennel Club: Delavan, Wisconsin

GM .... Green Mountain Race Track: Pownal, Vermont

GT .... Greentrack Greyhound Park: Eutaw, Alabama

HI .... Hinsdale Greyhound Park: Hinsdale, New Hampshire

HO .... Hollywood Greyhound Park: Hallandale, Florida

IS .... Interstate Greyhound Park: Byers, Colorado

JA .... Jacksonville Kennel Club: Jacksonville, Florida

JC .... Jefferson County Kennel Club: Monticello, Florida

KW .... Key West Greyhound Park: Key West, Florida

LI .... Lincoln Park (renamed Twin River): Lincoln, Rhode Island

LR .... Lakes Region Greyhound Park: Belmont, New Hampshire

LV .... Las Vegas Greyhound Park: Las Vegas, Nevada

MB .... Melbourne Greyhound Park: Melbourne, Florida

MH .... Mile High Greyhound Park: Commerce City, Colorado

MO .... Mobile Greyhound Park: Mobile, Alabama

MU	....	Multnomah Greyhound Park: Wood Village, Oregon
NF	....	Naples–Ft. Meyers Greyhound Track: Bonita Springs, Florida
OP	....	Orange Park Kennel Club: Jacksonville, Florida
PB	....	Palm Beach Kennel Club: West Palm Beach, Florida
PE	....	Pensacola Greyhound Track: Pensacola, Florida
PH	....	Phoenix Greyhound Park: Phoenix, Arizona
PL	....	Plainfield Greyhound Park: Plainfield, Connecticut
PU	....	Pueblo Greyhound Park: Pueblo, Colorado
RM	....	Rocky Mountain Greyhound Park: Colorado Springs, Colorado
RT	....	Raynham–Taunton Greyhound Park: Raynham, Massachusetts
SO	....	Sanford–Orlando Kennel Club: Longwood, Florida
SA	....	Sarasota Kennel Club: Sarasota, Florida
SE	....	Seabrook Greyhound Park: Seabrook, New Hampshire
SM	....	Seminole Greyhound Park: Casselberry, Florida
SS	....	Shoreline Star Greyhound Park: Bridgeport, Connecticut
SC	....	Sodrac Greyhound Park: North Sioux City, South Dakota
SL	....	Southland Greyhound Park: West Memphis, Arkansas
SJ	....	St. Johns Greyhound Park: Jacksonville, Florida
SP	....	Derby Lane (also known as St. Petersburg Kennel Club): St. Petersburg, Florida
ST	....	St. Croix Greyhound Racing: Hudson, Wisconsin
TP	....	Tampa Greyhound Track: Tampa, Florida
TR	....	Twin River (previously Lincoln Park): Lincoln, Rhode Island
TS	....	Tri-State Greyhound Park: Cross Lanes, West Virginia
TU	....	Tucson Greyhound Park: Tucson, Arizona
VG	....	Valley Race Park: Harlingen, Texas
VL	....	Victoryland Greyhound Park: Shorter, Alabama
WL	....	Waterloo Greyhound Park: Waterloo, Iowa
WD	....	Wheeling Downs (renamed Wheeling Island): Wheeling, West Virginia
WT	....	Wichita Greyhound Track: Valley Center, Kansas
WI	....	Wisconsin Dells Greyhound Park: Wisconsin Dells, Wisconsin
WO	....	Wonderland Greyhound Park: Revere, Massachusetts
WS	....	The Woodlands Kennel Club: Kansas City, Kansas
YU	....	Yuma Greyhound Park: Yuma, Arizona

Bibliography

Books

Blythe, Linda L. and James R Gannon. *Care of the Racing Greyhound: A Guide for Trainers, Breeders, and Veterinarians.* Abilene, KS: American Greyhound Council, 1994.

Hartwell, Paul C. *The Road From Emeryville: A History of Greyhound Racing.* Abilene, KS: National Greyhound Association, 2003.

Mueller, Georgiana. *How to Raise and Train a Greyhound.* Neptune City, NJ: TFH Publications, 1965.

Magazines

Britt, Shawni. "This Hall of Fame is Different." *National Greyhound Update*, November 1987.

Filipelli, Vera. "Derby Lane Turns 80." *The Greyhound Review*, January 2005.

Guccione, Gary. "Construction Starts in Abilene on Greyhound Hall of Fame." *The Greyhound Racing Record*, July 29, 1972.

Lebon, Gee. "Greyhounds as Pets." *Turnout*, February 1981.

Wooten, Leslie. "Beginnings." *The Greyhound Review*, September 2004.

———. "Growth." *The Greyhound Review*, October 2004.

———. "O.P. Smith in Tucson, 1910 Part I." *The Greyhound Review*, February 2005.

———. "O.P. Smith in Tucson, 1910 Part II." *The Greyhound Review*, March 2005.

Newspapers

Abilene Reflector-Chronicle, "Greyhound 'Super Stake' Set," October 9, 1975.

———, "K's Clown Breezes to Super Stake Win," November 14, 1975.

———, "Robber, Clown Head Field for Finals of Super Stake," November 11, 1975.

Barnett, Josephine. "Dog Track Backer Paints Rosy Picture," *Oregon Daily Journal*, January 18, 1963.

Boling, Dave. "Dogs Have Their Day in Grand Opening," *Spokane Spokesman Review*, August 22, 1988.

———. "Opener May Draw 5,000," *Spokane Spokesman Review*, August 21, 1988.

Cady, Steve. "Dog Days in Vermont," *New York Times*, August 10, 1975.

———. "Sports Betting Advocates Regrouping in Legislatures," *New York Times*, September 23, 1973.

Carberry, Jack. "$15,000 in Unredeemed Tickets at Mile High," *Denver Post*, April 13, 1955.

———. "New Pueblo Track Opens Next Monday," *Denver Post*, May 13, 1955.

Crist, Steven. "Dogs Biting Into Betting Dollars," *New York Times*, August 4, 1980.

———. "Dog Racing: Long Shot or Safe Bet?," *New York Times*, August 6, 1978.

———. "Plainfield Track Runs a Winning Streak," *New York Times*, July 16, 1978.

Dallas Morning News, "Beyond The Finish Effort Stepped-up to Find Homes for Retired Racing Greyhounds," March 28, 1993.

———, "The Dogs Have Their Day: Houston-Area Track a Howling Success," July 27, 1993.

Denver Post, "Alderson 'Jet' Cops Feature," May 28, 1955.

———, "Ancient Sport of Dog Racing New in Empire," July 17, 1949.

———, "Byers Dog Track to Make Debut," February 12, 1971.

———, "Cloverleaf Dog Track Schooling Races Near," April 24, 1955.

———, "Cloverleaf Opens Season Before 5,700 Fans," May 28, 1955.

———, "Crowd Wagers $53,950 at Mile High Dog Track," July, 29, 1949.

———, "Dogs Know More About Racing Than Customers Who Bet on Them," July 19, 1949.

———, "Dog Run Fast Times in Test," July 7, 1949.

———, "Dog Track Opens, Fans Bet $23,046," July 22, 1949.

———, "Early Arrivals at Mile High," May 22, 1955.

———, "Fans Wager $18,589 at Pueblo Dog Opener," July 16, 1949.

———, "Greyhound Marks Fall at Pueblo," July 22, 1949.

———, "Greyhound Racing Makes Colorado Debut at New Pueblo Track Tonight," July 15, 1949.

———, "Greyhound Schooling Races Start Under Lights Wednesday," July 10, 1949.

———, "Greyhounds to Run Under Lights Tonight," July 16, 1949.

———, "Inaugural Features Cloverleaf Program," May 27, 1955.

———, "Interstate Looks for Speedup," February 15, 1971.

———, "Mile High Spruces Up for '55 Meeting," May 5, 1955.

———, "Nine Swiftest Dogs to Run at Mile High," July 26, 1949.

———, "One of Nation's Top Greyhounds Arrives," July 3, 1949.

———, "Schooling Continues at Interstate Track," February 7, 1971.

———, "Schooling Starts at New Track," May 16, 1955.

———, "Sprint Slated in Dog Trials," February 3, 1971.

———, "State Control of Dogs Assures Honest Racing," July 20, 1949.

———, "Tote Board Delays Dog Track Opening," July 17, 1949.

———, "Wager Mark Set By Dog Betters," July 30, 1949.

——, "WeHo Wins Cloverleaf Feature in Record Time," May 31, 1955.

——, "World's Fastest Dogs Set for Denver Debut," July 24, 1949.

Gibbs, Shea W. "Let the Puppies Run," *Pinellas News*, January 9, 2004.

Grimaldi, Paul. "Greyhound Racing at Twin River in Lincoln Ends Saturday," *Providence Journal*, August 8, 2009.

Hamby, Bruce. "Denver Racing Due by 1949," *Denver Post*, November 3, 1948.

Henry, Mike. "Derby Lane Still Evolving with Weaver," *Bradenton Herald*, October 12, 2002.

Harvey, John. "ORC Delays Final Action," *Oregonian*, February 2, 1963.

Houston Chronicle, "Dog Racing Returns to Texas," November 15, 1990.

——, "Countdown for Dog Track La Marque Greyhound Park Opens in Nov.," July 10, 1992.

Kuempel, George. "Pari-Mutuel Dog Wagering Beats Horse Racing Out of Gate in Texas," *Dallas Morning News*, November 15, 1990.

Madden, Richard L. "Ansonia, Conn., in Surprise Vote, Spurns Proposed Greyhound Track," *New York Times*, January 15, 1979.

Matteucci, Megan. "The Rhode Island Greyhound Owners Association Gives $110,000 to 28 Local Charities, a Percentage of Dog-Owners' Purse," *Providence Journal*, November 24, 2002.

McLeod, Don. "Dog Meeting Due Monday," *Oregonian*, July 14, 1957.

——. "MKC track to be Renamed," *Oregonian*, August 17, 1978.

——. "Study Due Clackamas Dog Track," *Oregonian*, January 15, 1963.

New York Times, "2 Arrested at Dog Races," August 3, 1928.

——, "2 Borough Presidents Back Greyhound Racing for City," June 3, 1975.

——, "6 New Horse Tracks Licensed in Florida-Racing Commission Also Issues Permits to 14 New Dog Tracks for Winter Sports," July 26, 1932.

——, "300 Dogs to Open Race Meet Today," July 7, 1924.

——, "8,000 at Mineola as Dog Track Opens," June 21, 1934.

——, "12,000 See Greyhound Races," June 16, 1935.

——, "$10,000,000 at Stake in Florida Racing," January 10, 1927.

——, "All Racing Banned on Call of Byrnes to Aid War Effort," December 24, 1944.

——, "Another Dog Track Closes," January 23, 1928.

——, "Award Racing Dates for Florida Tracks," November 30, 1931.

——, "Bars Bet on Dog Races," July 27, 1924.

——, "Betting Bill Passed in Massachusetts," June 30, 1934.

——, "Conn. Licenses First Dog Track," September 18, 1974.

——, "Connecticut Dog Track is Approved," August 23, 1975.

——, "Connecticut Gaming Given Push," May 31, 1974.

——, "Court Sets Aside Racing Injunctions," January 25, 1927.

——, "Court Shuts Down Racing in Florida," March 10, 1927.

——, "Dog Races for Atlantic City," April 6, 1934.

——, "Dog Races Listed for Celtic Park," September 13, 1928.

——, "Dog Races Raided at Jersey Track," September 19, 1933.

——, "Dog Racers are Stranded," February 6, 1931.

——, "Dog Racers to Fight City," September 27, 1928.

——, "Dog Racing Banned in Jersey by Court," April 9, 1935.

——, "Dog Racing Minus Betting," January 6, 1928.

——, "Dog-Racing Wager Stay Denied; Called 'Scheme to Evade Law'," January 8, 1928.

——, "Dog Track Gets Building Go-Ahead," September 3, 1975.

——, "Dog Track in N.H. Sold for $870,000," April 10, 1976.

——, "Drive on Gambling Opens In Florida," February 1, 1929.

——, "F.B.I. Steps into Dog Racing Strike," March 26, 1975.

——, "Florida Backs Race Tax Split," November 8, 1940.

——, "Florida County Votes for Dog Races," November 4, 1931.

——, "Florida Foresees $30,000,000 Season," February 17, 1934.

——, "Florida Gets $1,421,205 from Racing, Jai Alai," April 12, 1936.

——, "Florida Racing Listed," July 16, 1942.

——, "Gov. Grasso Rules Out Funds for Ramps to Dog Track," January 10, 1976.

——, "Grand Jury Upholds Sale of Dog Photos," August 31, 1928.

——, "Greyhound Owners End Boycott," July 23, 1975.

——, "Greyhound Pays Record of $432," March 18, 1932.

——, "Greyhound Racing in America and England Organized Under One Large Association," March 5, 1926.

——, "Greyhound Sold for $60,000," June 1, 1979.

——, "Injunction is Denied Florida Dog Course," January 1, 1928.

——, "New Florida Commission Gets Four Race Track Applications," June 30, 1931.

——, "No Crime Ties to Dog Racing Found," July 26, 1975.

——, "Owners' Strike Closes Dog Racing Track," July 5, 1975.

——, "Palm Beach for Dog Races," November 25, 1931.

——, "Pari-Mutuel Betting on Dogs Illegal, Kentucky, Court Holds," February, 27, 1926.

——, "Police Raid Dog Track," July 26, 1929.

——, "Queens Dog Racing Delayed By Suits," September 28, 1928.

——, "Race Tracks Seek Dates in Florida," July 14, 1942.

———, "Racing Approved in Florida Voting," October 21, 1931.

———, "Racing Bill Favored," March 12, 1931.

———, "Racing Dogs Subpoenaed," July 23, 1931.

———, "Record Betting Weekend in Connecticut," July 8, 1976.

———, "Record Total Set in Florida Betting," April 3, 1934.

———, "Revenue of $1,018,140 from Florida Racing," January 26, 1942.

———, "Revere Seeks 100-Day Dog Meet," January 5, 1944.

———, "Rooney Family Seeking Connecticut Dog Track," March 15, 1978.

———, "Sheriff Halts Dog Races," June 11, 1935.

———, "Sheriffs Replace Lid on Ohio Racing," August 4, 1929.

———, "Ship Brings 72 Greyhounds," September 29, 1935.

———, "Striking Owners Sentenced," July 9, 1975.

———, "Striking Owners to Care for Dogs," July 6, 1975.

———, "Vinson Lifts Ban on Racing and Eliminates the Curfew," May 10, 1945.

———, "Votes for Pari-Mutuel Betting," March 11, 1931.

———, "Wars on Dog Race Gambling," August 15, 1926.

———, "Would End Dog Race Bets," June 24, 1930.

———, "Bus Service Due for Oval," July 7, 1957.

———, "Dog Racing Form Chart," August 12, 1933.

———, "Greyhound Racing to Start Tonight," May 25, 1933.

———, "Officials Ponder Dog Track Plan," February 2, 1963.

———, "Schooling Races for Dogs Start at Fairview Sunday," July 7, 1957.

Ortiz, Christopher. "Race is Over for Cloverleaf: Dog Track Closes Doors, McWhinney Looks to Swallow Property," *Greeley Tribune*, December 11, 2007.

Partner, Dan. "16, 328 at Mile High for Dog Inaugural," *Denver Post*, July 28, 1949.

Pasero, George. "Race Hearing Friday," *Oregon Daily Journal*, January 15, 1963.

Ripley, Anthony. "2D Arizonian Quits State Racing Unit," *New York Times*, December 6, 1970.

Spokane Spokesman Review, "Greyhounds Off and Running," August 21, 1988.

Strauss, Michael. "Florida Dog Races Lure Women Fans," *New York Times*, April 21, 1974.

Swing, William. "Racing Group Cancels Meet on New Plant," *Oregonian*, January 17, 1963.

Tolf, Robert. "The Florida Action: Fast Dogs, Frontons," *New York Times*, March 16, 1975.

Tomasson, Robert. "Dog Track a Leader in Bets," *New York Times*, October 26, 1980.

Torbenson, Eric. "Dog Racing Reaches Finish Line," *Spokane Spokesman Review*,
     December 18, 1995.

Wichita Eagle, "KC Races Draw 6,203 Usual Opening Woes Occur," September 15, 1989.

Wreschner, Jeff. "Racing dogs Are a Passion for Fulchinos," *Norwich Bulletin*,
     December 29, 2003.

Zerner, Charles. "New Jersey Finds Dog Races Illegal," *New York Times*,
     September 30, 1934.

Other Periodicals

Galloway, Melissa. "Adopt a Grey." *Greyhounds*: Popular Dogs Series no. 20 (2001): 50–59.

McCullough, Susan. "The Original Dog." *Greyhounds*: Popular Dogs Series
     no. 20 (2001): 10–17.

Thornton, Kim. "Greyhound Racing." *Greyhounds*: Popular Dogs Series
     no. 20 (2001): 34–45.

Video Recording

1945–1995: Celebrating 50 Years in Abilene, Kansas, special ed. VHS. National Greyhound
     Association, 1995.

Ensuring the Welfare of the Racing Greyhound, special ed. VHS. American Greyhound
     Council, 2003.

Discover Wisconsin Greyhounds, special ed. VHS. HVS Productions, 1990.

Greyhound: The Life of an Athlete, special ed. VHS. Brava Films, 2003.

Greyhound Racing: *The History & Heart of the Sport*, special ed. VHS. Greyhound Hall of
     Fame, 2001.

Sprint Through History, special ed. VHS. Greyhound Hall of Fame, 1987.

Track 75 Years of Racing, special ed. VHS. Greyhound Hall of Fame, 2003.

Special Thanks

A special thanks goes to the following people for sharing their time and knowledge with me: June Bazar, David Blair, Linda Lou Blythe, Sally Briggs, Richard Brindle, Darrel Brumage, Peggy Brumage, Jack Butler, Mary Butler, Timothy Cahill, Joe Calabro, Sue Calabro, Don Conatser, Judy Enyart, Francesca Field, John Filipelli, Vera Filipelli, Maurice Flynn Jr., Frederick Fulchino, Jim Gartland, Gil Gilley, Kathleen Gilley, Cheryl Gilson, Rory Gorée, Jeff Gubbels, Stacy Gubbels, Gary Guccione, John Hern Jr., Sharon Holder, Tim Horan, Herb "Dutch" Koerner, Patti Lehnert, Connie Loebsack, Kathy Lounsbury, Donna Lovely, John Manning, Charles Marriott, Dennis McKeon, Donna Moore, Lois Mowery, Cynthia O'Conner, David Peck, Janele Peck, Craig Randle, Harry Rogers, Shirley Rogers, Dan Ryan, Elizabeth Sanders, Kirk Schaffer, Lisa Schaffer, Ed Scheele, Jacques Triplett, Ann Waitley, Deneen Ward, Wayne Ward, Diane Whiteley, Carl Wilson, Jan Woll.

Having raced only seventeen times, three-year-old Mocha (Bit The Bullet–PU) enjoys her all-too-sudden retirement in Auburn, Washington. While the pup could run fast, she was unfortunately disqualified for being too aggressive with other Greyhounds while racing.

Index

Note
Page numbers in bold indicate photographs.